50 STRATEGIES for Learning without Screens

Tom Rademacher, M.Ed.

To my students, because some piece of every one of you taught me to teach.

—TR

Publishing Credits

Corinne Burton, M.A.Ed., *President and Publisher*
Aubrie Nielsen, M.S.Ed., *EVP of Content Development*
Kyra Ostendorf, M.Ed., *Publisher, professional books*
Véronique Bos, *VP of Creative*
Christine Zuchora-Walske, *Senior Editorial Manager*
Kevin Pham, *Graphic Designer*
Emily R. Smith, M.A.Ed., *SVP of Content Development*
Leslie Reichert, *Content Manager*

Image Credits

All images from iStock and/or Shutterstock

Library of Congress Cataloging-in-Publication Data

Names: Rademacher, Tom, 1981- author.
Title: 50 strategies for learning without screens / Tom Rademacher.
Other titles: Fifty strategies for learning without screens
Description: Huntington Beach, CA : Shell Educational Publishing, Inc, 2024. | Includes bibliographical references.
Identifiers: LCCN 2024005254 (print) | LCCN 2024005255 (ebook) | ISBN 9798765965733 (paperback) | ISBN 9798765965740 (ebook) | ISBN 9798765965757 (epub)
Subjects: LCSH: Learning strategies. | Effective teaching. | Individualized instruction. | BISAC: EDUCATION / Teaching / Methods & Strategies | EDUCATION / General
Classification: LCC LB1066 .R34 2024 (print) | LCC LB1066 (ebook) | DDC 371.102--dc23/eng/20240403
LC record available at https://lccn.loc.gov/2024005254
LC ebook record available at https://lccn.loc.gov/2024005255

Shell Education

A division of Teacher Created Materials
5482 Argosy Avenue
Huntington Beach, CA 92649
www.tcmpub.com/shell-education
ISBN 979-8-7659-6573-3
© 2025 Shell Educational Publishing, Inc.
Printed by: **51307**
Printed In: **USA**
PO#: **12476**

Table of Contents

Introduction

Strategies

Appendices

Welcome

I love screens. If I used every computer, phone, TV, and tablet in my home, I could set up a wall of screens playing fifteen different Marvel movies at once. And if I set them up in release order, I would only get to *Guardians of the Galaxy Volume 2*. Maybe I need more screens.

In other words: I'm not an antiscreen evangelist. This book is not an argument to remove all computers or destroy all smartphones (although there are days when I wish the internet had an off button). I know that for many students and teachers, technology gives access to ideas, opportunities, and connections that would otherwise be inaccessible—and would have been unimaginable thirty years ago.

Rather, I'm sharing strategies for teaching and learning without screens so you can help the kids in front of you live, work, and thrive in a tech-rich world. To do this, students need skills that are best taught without screens. They need to learn what they can do, what they can notice, and what they can wonder about so they can use screens in creative, productive, and participatory ways, rather than simply as consumers of media.

Screens make it easy to *watch* instead of *make*; to outsource questions instead of wondering about them. In the use of any educational technology, the most important element is the brain of the person using it. Who's in charge—the brain or the tech? Is the brain curious, creative, critical, collaborative, and compassionate? If yes, then the tech is a tool for doing something better and more beautifully than the tech could do on its own. Is the brain passive, simply being told or entertained? If so, then the tech is keeping the student quiet, but not helping them learn.

When I reflect on the days, lessons, and moments in my sixteen years of teaching that were most impactful, most memorable, or most important, I notice that screens were hardly ever involved. I've collected my own favorite screen-free teaching strategies here, as well as some from trusted colleagues from across the country. I hope these fifty strategies will engage your students, inspire critical and creative thinking, and help your students tackle complex ideas in ways that are meaningful, joyful, enjoyable, engaging, and challenging. You can adapt these strategies across subjects, abilities, and grade levels.

I can't imagine what our world will look like when today's students are grown, watching *Guardians of the Galaxy Volume 12: Naptime after a Big Dinner* projected from a microchip in their wallet to a receiver tucked into their ocular nerves. Okay, I guess I *can* imagine it, though I'm no doubt getting it all wrong. I'm confident, though, that the world *will* get increasingly digital. A student's ability to navigate that digital world will be the key predictor of their success. This is exactly why educators need to get the screens off students' desks and out of their hands as often as possible.

Going Old School to Be Future Ready

Wherever students end up, and whatever they end up doing, their abilities to think critically and creatively, to work with a wide range of people, and to adapt to changing circumstances will be crucial. Experts in the fields of education and economics agree that this group of skills—whether we call them "twenty-first-century skills," "soft skills," "applied digital skills," or "what good teaching has sought to do since forever"—is essential (Appleby 2017; World Economic Forum 2023; OECD 2019; Partnership for 21st Century Learning 2015). Young people will need more human than digital skills to navigate their future.

If you're looking for more details about these skills and why they're important, I recommend reading three foundational documents, described in the following list and in the tables on the next page.

- One of my favorite reports on digital media and learning was led by Henry Jenkins when he was working as the director of the Comparative Media Studies Program at Massachusetts Institute of Technology (MIT). This report discusses the tools young people need to shift from cultural bystanders to cultural participants. He calls those tools "**new media literacies**" (Jenkins 2009). Jenkins says that in spaces asking users to simply consume, it's important and powerful to do more: to create and participate. He also notes ethical concerns about who is taught to participate. For example, if some students use their school devices to learn coding or film production and editing while other students use their devices mainly as digital worksheet machines, there's an equity problem to solve that goes beyond access to technology. Some students are being denied opportunities to create.

- The most widely referenced document on **twenty-first-century learning** skills was first released in 2006 by the Partnership for 21st Century Learning, which brought together education and business leaders to discuss the essential skills of a future workforce (Partnership for 21st Century Learning 2015). Honestly, the term *twenty-first-century skills* has always seemed a little silly to me because most of these skills have always been and will always be important. But while I don't love the name, I do endorse the skills this document lists.

- A third framework is more concise and has a name I really like. The Deeper Learning framework offers a set of competencies that "students must master in order to develop a keen understanding of academic content and apply their knowledge to problems in the classroom and on the job" (William and Flora Hewlett Foundation 2013). I like the **deeper learning competencies** because they apply across grade levels and disciplines, and I think they put into context a lot of the work that teachers know to be important.

New Media Literacies

Play	Distributed cognition	Negotiation
Performance	Collective intelligence	Appropriation
Simulation	Transmedia navigation	Judgment
Multitasking	Networking	

Framework for 21st Century Learning

Learning and innovation skills:

- creativity and innovation
- critical thinking and problem-solving
- communication and collaboration
- information

Information and technology skills:

- information literacy
- media literacy
- information and communications technology literacy

Life and career skills:

- flexibility and adaptability
- initiative and self-direction
- social and cross-cultural skills
- productivity and accountability
- leadership and responsibility

Deeper Learning Competencies

Master core academic content	Work collaboratively
Think critically and solve complex problems	Learn how to learn
Communicate effectively	Develop academic mindsets

There's probably little here to surprise you. These foundational documents are all more than ten years old, and most of the skills they list have been important for much longer than that. These skills were nearly all crucial to celebrated geniuses like Leonardo da Vinci (artist and polymath), Marie Curie (physicist and chemist), and Gallagher (smasher of watermelons).

What You'll Find in This Book

I've taken bits from all three frameworks to organize the strategies in this book into these sections:

 Thinking Curiously

 Thinking Creatively

 Thinking Critically

 Thinking Compassionately

 Thinking Collaboratively

Thinking Curiously: Learning to Learn

Anticipating rewarding information

The strategies in this section do not teach curiosity so much as they seek to inspire it and give it room and reason in your classroom, to hook students on the feeling of anticipating rewarding information. The link between curiosity and learning is an important one. One analysis of research on brain science and curiosity concluded that "curiosity states elicit activity in the brain's dopaminergic circuit and thereby enhance hippocampus-dependent learning for information associated with high curiosity but also for incidental information encountered during high-curiosity states" (Gruber, Valji, and Ranganath 2017). In other words, curiosity helps you see things you don't understand yet. It helps you learn unexpected things as you chase your questions like rabbits through the forest. Curiosity is "the anticipation of rewarding information" (Loewenstein 1994).

Thinking Critically: Learning to Read the Unwritten

Resolving states of doubt and doubting states of belief

The strategies in this section help students apply reason and question assumptions to solve problems, analyze information, and discern biases. Critical thinking scholar James Southworth says critical thinking is both moving "from a confirmed belief to a position of doubt" and "resolving states of doubt" (Southworth 2022, para. 1–2).

Critical thinking is . . . well, thinking hard. However, teaching critical thinking is not as easy as standing in front of the class and telling students, "Think harder!" (I've tried that, and it didn't work.) To engage in critical thinking, students must first build basic skills; an understanding of fact, opinion, and personal perspective; and a habit of questioning new information (Dwyer 2023).

Thinking Collaboratively: Learning from Each Other

Moving together like dancers

In the field of collective neuroscience, researchers study how shared experiences cause "neurons in corresponding locations of the different brains [to] fire at the same time, creating matching patterns, like dancers moving together" (Denworth 2023, para. 2). When brains dance together, people learn better. A recent study attached a teacher and four students to electroencephalograms (EEGs) and recorded not just how each person's brain reacted to learning, but how their brain waves began to mirror and respond to one another. It found that when "brain synchrony" happens because of shared learning, students not only learn better in the moment, but also remember more much later (Davidesco et al. 2023).

If anyone is dreaming of the day when schools involve isolated spaces for each student to learn independently on an artificial intelligence (AI)–driven digital platform, well, I am happy to burst that particularly dystopian bubble. It turns out that not only do humans need to learn to work together, but they also learn better together. Relationships aid learning and make learning more meaningful. The strategies in this section provide opportunities for students to learn with and from each other, to practice communicating and solving problems in groups, and to share memorable experiences in your classroom.

Thinking Creatively: Learning to Make

Imagining a novel and specific future

One study on divergent thinking (a type of creative thinking) describes it as "the ability to imagine novel and specific future autobiographical events" (Thakral et al. 2021, para. 1). The strategies in this section are all about creating space, support, and inspiration for students to make new things—to imagine a future and the steps needed to build it.

Of all the things that computers can't do, creativity is the one thing computers can't do the most. Sure, they can piece together bits from all over into something that appears to be new, but humans have cornered the market on making entirely new things, having entirely new ideas, and writing entirely new stories. Creative thinking builds every bit of what's next.

Thinking Compassionately: Learning with Care

Collective noticing to promote healing

A 2023 meta-analysis of 424 studies supported programs of social-emotional learning in which all adults and students are taught to recognize, communicate, and coregulate emotions; accept responsibility for feelings of safety of everyone; and communicate with and learn from people in an open, respectful way. Schools that implemented such programs saw increases not only in students' emotional well-being, but also in their academic success (Cipriano et. al 2023). Social-emotional learning is often directed at individual skills, but helping students see and understand every person's role in a compassionate culture is equally important. Compassionate culture, or organizational compassion, is a "collective noticing, feeling, and responding to suffering that promotes healing" (Kanov et al. 2004, as cited in Mascaro et al. 2020). The strategies in this section will help students develop a more complete understanding of their own identities and those of others; the social, emotional, and cultural competencies needed to understand multiple perspectives; and tools to act in compassionate ways toward the world around them.

Tips for Teaching a Constantly Connected Generation

A survey by the EdWeek Research Center showed that prepandemic, 66 percent of secondary schools had one-to-one devices, and 42 percent of elementary schools did. By 2021 those numbers had soared to 90 percent of secondary schools and 84 percent of elementary schools (Klein 2021). The return to in-person learning hasn't reduced classroom usage of screens. One report showed a doubling of the number of separate educational technology tools from 2020 to 2022 (Styers 2022). In other words: counting all the laptops, projectors, interactive whiteboards, phones, tablets, and smart watches, many classrooms have more total screens than eyeballs.

> ### Quick Tech Inventory
> - On a typical day, how many screens are in your room, counting school and personal devices (everyone's devices, not just yours)?
> - What activities are screens used for during the school day?
> - How many of the skills being taught in screen-based activities actually require screens?
> - What percentage of work on which students are assessed in your class is done digitally?

Teaching Tech-Attached Kids

I use the term *tech-attached* because I really struggle with using *addiction* to describe how students feel about their phones, games, and tablets. Addiction as a diagnosis has a specific set of parameters and behaviors that I have no expertise in, and the impacts are so serious that it's just one of those words I try not to use casually. But I get it. Attachment can look like addiction, especially when a phone cannot be put down or a game cannot be turned off even though everyone is at the door waiting and we're going to be late and it's just a video game not real life and Grandma is *waiting for us*!

A recent meta-analysis of research on interventions for children and adolescents with digital addictions recommends cognitive behavioral therapy, pharmacology, family therapy, and physical exercise—all of which are beyond the scope of educators

(Ding and Li 2023). Embedded within these broader recommendations are more specific components such as reducing time online, creating a healthy internet-use schedule, and understanding the forces that drive internet overuse.

You can't control how and when your students use screens when they aren't in your school. You probably have your hands full trying to keep them off screens when they're right in front of you. There's no perfect solution here. As with most big problems in education, this one's solution includes: build healthy relationships, do your best to help it get better, fail a lot, and keep trying. Check out Common Sense Education (commonsense.org/education) for free K–12 curriculum to help students build essential digital habits and skills.

Planning Lessons in Chunks

One thing I learned during my classroom teaching years was that the harder I worked to build a lesson with complex structure and teaching technique, the more likely it was to blow up in my face. Put another way, improving education is not as simple as choosing one technique over another. One study found that when considering just fifteen instructional techniques with various dosage levels and choices for early and late instruction, there were 205 trillion instructional options available (Koedinger, Booth, and Klahr 2013). That is a lot of options. So what can you do? Rather than mixing, matching, and stacking styles and substance, plan your lessons in smaller, clearer chunks with obvious goals.

Paper Is Good for You

For many years, I taught the graphic novel *MAUS* to my eighth graders alongside Gregory Stanton's Ten Stages of Genocide, looking at how language is used to categorize, dehumanize, and polarize populations. We used digital copies of the book, and I thought students would love being able to zoom, click through, and use their computers to read it. I had a few paper copies around for when someone forgot to charge their laptop. I noticed that every single hour, those books were snatched up before the bell rang.

There's just something about books. You get it. I get it. My students got it.

Research shows that reading on paper is better than reading on screens in many ways. Here are just a few:

- Children showed lower reading performance when reading on screens (Furenes, Kucirkova, and Bus 2021).

- Students with attention deficit hyperactivity disorder (ADHD) showed much higher comprehension and spent more time reading when reading on paper (Ben-Yehudah and Brann 2019).

Tips for Teaching Tech-Attached Kids

- Teach how algorithms and brain chemistry work.
- Show students how to turn off notifications (and how to communicate this change to their friends and family members).
- Invite students to share their strategies for when they're getting overwhelmed by digital information.
- Teach and model skills for consciously unplugging; encourage choice over command.

Chunking Tips

- Keep it simple.
- Keep it short.
- Keep it clear.

- The physical acts of holding and turning the pages of a book strengthened the neural pathways needed to read in a way that screen time did not (Horowitz-Kraus and Hutton 2018).

- Reading on paper correlated with more energy in higher-frequency bands of brain waves (associated with concentration and visual attention) than screen reading did because "children's attention is overloaded when exposed to screens" (Zivan et al. 2023, para. 26).

Of course, these findings are just pieces in a puzzle that also includes the fact that I read all this research on a screen where I was able to follow hyperlinks, easily look up big words I didn't know, and get access to documents I would never have had in my house. Not to mention the fact that I've witnessed kids (my own included) making huge leaps in literacy because of text- and reading-rich games, because the engagement is so high in games, and also because they think books are for nerds.

I could fill pages and pages with research evidence on the value of paper and physical writing for collaboration, creativity, note-taking, and problem-solving. Of course computers have a role to play in how people read, write, and work together, but it's obvious students need plenty of time to experience folded corners, pencil smudges, and doodles in the margins of whatever they're reading.

Giving Students Freedom

The *Journal of Pediatrics* published a study that found a decrease in independent activity is a "primary cause of the rise in mental disorders" in children (Gray, Lancy, and Bjorklund 2023, para. 3). The study points out that from 1950 to 2010, the average school year grew by five weeks. In addition, modern culture increasingly discourages children from exploring the world on their own. As a result, today's young people have a distinct lack of freedom to play.

That same study also has good news, though: teachers can help. The authors found that students involved in activities that were "like play" (offered as a choice and without close adult supervision) were more engaged, smiled more, and were more physically active (Gray, Lancy, and Bjorklund 2023). If young people need more freedom and are spending more and more time in school, teachers can make their classrooms places where young people experience more freedom more often.

Smarter Than the Internet

I once attended a meeting in which a district leader explained why libraries were a thing of the past. We were gathered in a library, a room that felt magical to me, a place that told every person who entered, "I love you

> ### Tips for Reading and Writing on Paper
>
> - Make books available and plentiful.
> - Create a practice of writing notes and ideas on paper.
> - Offer printed copies of in-class and at-home reading.
> - Talk with students about how and why reading on paper feels different from reading on screens.

> ### Tips for Increasing Freedom
>
> - Add choice to in-class work.
> - Give autonomy in how and where students use their time.
> - Let students know you trust them without constantly surveilling them.
> - Let students play without telling them what to play.

so much that you can read all my books for free." The idea of a library is just one of those things that feel too cool to be real but are actually real. Like narwhals.

The guy leading the meeting held up his phone and said, "Why do we need a whole library when everything in this room is in this phone?" It was a silly thing to say, because for one thing he was ignoring the existence of librarians, and for another, he was just deeply wrong. The internet is pretty neat, but it's not a place that does what libraries do. The online world is a place of ideas, but hardly ever of nuance. Finding answers in a library may take more work than asking the internet, but those library answers will probably be more complete, be more complex, and lead to bigger or better questions.

And yet these days when most people have a question, their first instinct is to ask the internet. Sometimes it works. If you're asking *when* the Battle of Gettysburg happened, the internet will deliver. If you're asking *why* it happened, the internet kinda stinks. Likewise, if you want to understand why the Gettysburg Address is one of the most famous speeches in US history even though Abraham Lincoln took only two minutes to say it, you're going to need something a whole lot smarter than the internet, such as a room full of twelve-year-olds. This is not a joke. I've experienced few things in my life that are as insightful, imaginative, and inspired as a room of middle schoolers thinking hard about how things work.

It is your responsibility to show the young people in your care that they are smarter *by far* than the internet. They are capable of great things—of empathy and creativity and humanity—that no screen can give them. The next Gettysburg Address can't be found on Google and won't be written by AI. Who will write it if today's young people aren't building their own brilliant answers to the hardest questions we can give them?

How to Use This Resource

Choose a strategy and give it a try! You can use the strategies exactly as they are or modify them to suit your students' unique needs. All the strategies in this book can be expanded or adapted to fit many grade levels and topics.

All strategies share additional tips or resources to support continued learning on the topic.

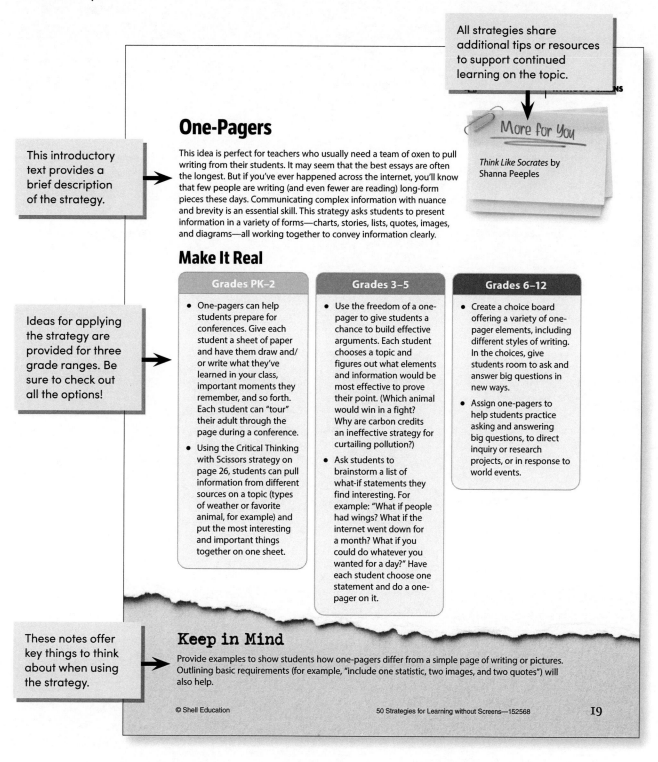

This introductory text provides a brief description of the strategy.

One-Pagers

This idea is perfect for teachers who usually need a team of oxen to pull writing from their students. It may seem that the best essays are often the longest. But if you've ever happened across the internet, you'll know that few people are writing (and even fewer are reading) long-form pieces these days. Communicating complex information with nuance and brevity is an essential skill. This strategy asks students to present information in a variety of forms—charts, stories, lists, quotes, images, and diagrams—all working together to convey information clearly.

More for You

Think Like Socrates by Shanna Peeples

Make It Real

Ideas for applying the strategy are provided for three grade ranges. Be sure to check out all the options!

Grades PK–2

- One-pagers can help students prepare for conferences. Give each student a sheet of paper and have them draw and/or write what they've learned in your class, important moments they remember, and so forth. Each student can "tour" their adult through the page during a conference.

- Using the Critical Thinking with Scissors strategy on page 26, students can pull information from different sources on a topic (types of weather or favorite animal, for example) and put the most interesting and important things together on one sheet.

Grades 3–5

- Use the freedom of a one-pager to give students a chance to build effective arguments. Each student chooses a topic and figures out what elements and information would be most effective to prove their point. (Which animal would win in a fight? Why are carbon credits an ineffective strategy for curtailing pollution?)

- Ask students to brainstorm a list of what-if statements they find interesting. For example: "What if people had wings? What if the internet went down for a month? What if you could do whatever you wanted for a day?" Have each student choose one statement and do a one-pager on it.

Grades 6–12

- Create a choice board offering a variety of one-pager elements, including different styles of writing. In the choices, give students room to ask and answer big questions in new ways.

- Assign one-pagers to help students practice asking and answering big questions, to direct inquiry or research projects, or in response to world events.

These notes offer key things to think about when using the strategy.

Keep in Mind

Provide examples to show students how one-pagers differ from a simple page of writing or pictures. Outlining basic requirements (for example, "include one statistic, two images, and two quotes") will also help.

© Shell Education   50 Strategies for Learning without Screens—152568   19

Strategies Table of Contents

Graphic Novels and Comic Strips

Find your school librarian. (If you don't have one, put this book down, run for office, send money to school libraries, then come back.) Ask them what part of the library is most popular with students. They will probably tell you it's the graphic novel section. (If your library doesn't have a graphic novel section, well, you know what to do.) Librarians know that graphic novels provide high-interest reading, build content knowledge, and offer human perspectives on historical events. But the graphic novel or comic strip as a writing style is often overlooked as a way for students to show their own thinking and learning about a topic or skill. Give students blank paper and comic templates, rulers, art supplies, and a few simple comic samples to look through, and they will reward you with original and engaged thinking.

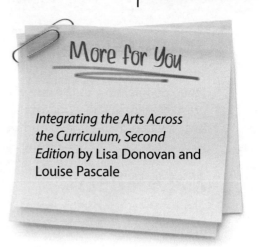

More for You

Integrating the Arts Across the Curriculum, Second Edition by Lisa Donovan and Louise Pascale

Make It Real

Grades PK–2	Grades 3–5	Grades 6–12
• On the board or on chart paper, draw a simple comic with no words. Have students come up with their own stories based on what you draw. • After reading a story out loud, give each student a sheet of paper printed with three blank comic panels and ask them to draw three parts of the story.	• Students can use comic templates to draw summaries of important events, math or science concepts, or the plots of stories they have read. • When studying parts of a story or an aspect of writing, students can show mastery by drawing their own comics that illustrate one or more key terms.	• Graphic novels make an inclusive alternative or addition to a research project. Each student can choose the perspective of one person involved and tell all or some of their story to humanize a complex or wide-ranging event. • Quick comics of stick figures and labeled drawings help students rehearse and review difficult concepts in a new way.

Keep in Mind

Not everyone is a skilled visual artist. If you are grading or assessing comics in any way, be clear that you are grading on the learning and thinking they show, not on artistic talent (unless that talent is one of your lesson's essential skills). You can also give students options to draw simple images, create collages, or work in teams with students who have a variety of skills.

Math Art

Some people, such as the one writing this book, find it hard to grasp new math concepts without applying or visualizing them in a way that doesn't need numbers. You can use art to design or visualize a concept that introduces or reinforces foundational math.

More for You

Integrating the Arts in Mathematics, Second Edition by Linda Dacey and Lisa Donovan

Make It Real

Grades PK–2

- Geometric shapes are helpful for understanding symmetry and negative space. Students can fold sheets of paper in half, cut out half a shape on the fold, and then unfold the cutout to show symmetry. Or they can cut out shapes and use the shapes and their matching holes to show a negative-space version of symmetry.

- Display images of a variety of artworks and challenge students to find geometric shapes in the art. See how many they can find. As students get better at recognizing subtle shapes in images, give them their own copies of artworks and have them use pencils, crayons, or markers to outline the shapes they see.

Grades 3–5

- Have students work in teams. Each team uses a bright flashlight to cast the shadow of a small geometric shape on a sheet of paper tacked or taped to the wall. One student traces the shadow on the paper with a pencil or marker. First, challenge students to estimate how much larger the shadow is than the shape, then have them measure both and use multiplication and division to determine scale.

- Professional artists often use math for proportions, scaling, and symmetry. Show students a few famous examples (such as da Vinci, Escher, and Kandinsky), and have them create their own art using these math concepts.

Grades 6–12

- Creating visuals can help students understand why and how to balance atoms in a chemical equation by drawing them out (or using shapes to represent them), or using images rather than letter variables to practice algebra. (If two Godzillas equal ten sasquatches, and two sasquatches equal . . . you get the point.)

- Show examples of fractals created by computers and by nature, then have students develop algorithms they use to create their own fractal art.

Keep in Mind

You may hear a lot of "I thought this was math class" when you start doing new creative math projects with students. You may even get resistance that this isn't "real math." Explain how these projects work the math muscles in students' brains and show that math is everywhere.

One-Pagers

This idea is perfect for teachers who usually need a team of oxen to pull writing from their students. It may seem that the best essays are often the longest. But if you've ever happened across the internet, you'll know that few people are writing (and even fewer are reading) long-form pieces these days. Communicating complex information with nuance and brevity is an essential skill. This strategy asks students to present information in a variety of forms—charts, stories, lists, quotes, images, and diagrams—all working together to convey information clearly.

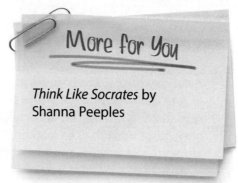

More for You

Think Like Socrates by Shanna Peeples

Make It Real

Grades PK–2

- One-pagers can help students prepare for conferences. Give each student a sheet of paper and have them draw and/or write what they've learned in your class, important moments they remember, and so forth. Each student can "tour" their adult through the page during a conference.

- Using the Critical Thinking with Scissors strategy on page 26, students can pull information from different sources on a topic (types of weather or favorite animal, for example) and put the most interesting and important things together on one sheet.

Grades 3–5

- Use the freedom of a one-pager to give students a chance to build effective arguments. Each student chooses a topic and figures out what elements and information would be most effective to prove their point. (Which animal would win in a fight? Why are carbon credits an ineffective strategy for curtailing pollution?)

- Ask students to brainstorm a list of what-if statements they find interesting. For example: "What if people had wings? What if the internet went down for a month? What if you could do whatever you wanted for a day?" Have each student choose one statement and do a one-pager on it.

Grades 6–12

- Create a choice board offering a variety of one-pager elements, including different styles of writing. In the choices, give students room to ask and answer big questions in new ways.

- Assign one-pagers to help students practice asking and answering big questions, to direct inquiry or research projects, or in response to world events.

Keep in Mind

Provide examples to show students how one-pagers differ from a simple page of writing or pictures. Outlining basic requirements (for example, "include one statistic, two images, and two quotes") will also help.

Writing Prompts

A consistent practice of freewriting or journaling is a powerful way to build a culture of writing in your classroom. Written responses to articles, lessons, or research can help students remember what they've learned. The right prompts enable students to access deep and original thinking.

More for You

The Write Thing by Kwame Alexander

Make It Real

Grades PK–2	Grades 3–5	Grades 6–12
• Sentence stems support young writers to dig deep and write complex ideas. In a group of stems, switch up the ideas and sentence parts left open. For example: "When I look at the stars, I think _____." And: "I feel _____ when I listen to music."	• When studying a historic event or movement or while reading a shared novel, ask students to write from the point of view of someone whose voice isn't heard in the materials at hand. What would they be thinking? Why? How do the happenings affect them?	• Ask your students to remember a conflict from their lives, your studies, or even from popular media and write an inner monologue for one person on each side of that conflict. Encourage students to try to understand what each person believed and why.
• Writing doesn't have to be written. In fact, many writers do their best writing while walking and talking or walking and thinking. Take your students on a story walk. Pair them up and have partners tell each other stories while they walk outdoors.	• Writing poorly can be really freeing. Ask students to write the worst poem, story, or joke they possibly can.	• A story walk (see Grades PK–2) can work well for secondary students too. For a more solo version, have each student carry a notebook on the walk and stop at a given point or at your signal to write down what they've been thinking about.

Keep in Mind

If students will be keeping their freewriting in the room and handing it in, have a discussion with them about privacy. Be honest with them about if and/or how often you will read what they've written, as they may have something they really do—or don't—want you to read.

Historical Primary Sources

I was once part of a teacher group on a special tour of a museum devoted to space travel (cool). During the tour, we were offered a choice: participate in a focus group session for a sponsor's new "virtual teacher" (less cool) or attend a presentation of documents from the archives (cooler than cool). I skipped the focus group and got to see primary sources such as handwritten letters from astronauts to administrators, lab notes from physicists, and concept drawings from old missions (the nerdiest cool). No matter the subject, primary sources exist online, in books, and in museums with curators dying to show them to curious kids.

More for You

Primary Source Readers: Around the World by Teacher Created Materials; Letters of Note (lettersofnote.com)

Make It Real

Grades PK–2	Grades 3–5	Grades 6–12
• Artifacts that students can touch and explore have a lot of impact. A great primary source doesn't need to be the original Declaration of Independence. Owner's manuals, magazines, photos, or comic books from Ye Olden Times (the 1980s) can be cheap, easy to find, and fun to explore. • Showing students copies of original handwritten drafts of stories they've read or songs they've heard can make history feel real and personal.	• Contact your local history museum, city hall, or historical society to schedule a guest speaker or a visit and get primary sources from around your area in the hands of your students. • Many primary sources related to topics in your curriculum are likely to be a challenge for students to read. The Collaborative Reading strategy on page 40 may help students tackle complex texts.	• Websites like Letters of Note offer primary source documents that show the personality and humanity of famous and not-so-famous people in history. These documents can make what you are studying feel more real to your students when they are given paper copies they can explore. • Primary sources are a great way to get students to fact-check common misconceptions or oversimplifications. Ask students questions like "What did that person actually say?" and "What came before or after that notable quote?"

Keep in Mind

Language in primary source documents may be out of date for any number of reasons. As much as possible, preview the sources students will have access to and be sure to discuss beforehand what they might see and why students should not repeat some things out loud.

Dynamic Diorama

Remember making dioramas for school with a bunch of dinosaurs or . . . was it ever anything besides dinosaurs? Anyway, this isn't that. A dynamic diorama involves students up and moving, using their bodies to create a diorama that represents a piece of a story, an idea, a feeling, or a question. Start simple by having a group of students reenact a painting or picture. As students grow more comfortable and confident in the strategy, you can make the prompts more complex or abstract.

More for you

You can team this strategy with the Picture Detectives strategy on page 31 to get students engaging with an idea in a visual and verbal way.

Make It Real

Grades PK–2	Grades 3–5	Grades 6–12
• Group students into lines in your gathering space and read a story. Pause after each page of the story (or after math problems that ask things like which is more, longer, or taller, etc.) to have one group silently create a diorama of what happened, hold for three breaths, then sit down. The next group takes a turn after the next page. • Give the student at the front of each line the role of director. The director tells group members where and how to position themselves. That student moves to the end of the line after the group creates its diorama.	• When working on a concept like tone, play different kinds of music and have each small group of students make a diorama that looks like the music feels to them. Each group can take turns showing and/or explaining their diorama. • You can use this strategy as a quick learning assessment. Instead of asking for a raised-hand verbal response to a question, ask if four or five students could show their understanding to the class as a diorama.	• Dioramas can be done in progressions to show connections between ideas, data points, or concepts. For example, dioramas can progressively convey related words (*mad*, *angry*, and *furious*) or different states of matter (ice, water, and vapor). • When students are being introduced to more complex or abstract mathematical concepts (showing the difference between volume and surface area, proportional relationships, or linear functions), dioramas can be used to model these concepts in a physical, active way.

Keep in Mind

Not every student will be comfortable in front of the class, especially when doing something that involves their body. You may want to talk with your students about being thoughtful with their comments to each other and have opportunities ready for students to participate as directors or in other nonperforming roles.

Pick Your Path

Remember those books where you got to the bottom of the page and had a choice to make about what to do next, and then usually you just ended up dying in a pit of snakes? Students can recreate that same level of fun with sticky notes and a wall or table. By adding options that lead down different paths, students can plan and read stories in an interactive way. You can use the same method to have students create classification systems, behavior expectations, and more.

More for You

Choose Your Own Adventure® books (cyoa.com)

Make It Real

Grades PK–2

- Create a fill-in-the-blanks story with blanks representing people, places, describing words, and so on. Invite each student to choose a word card for each category. Then, as you read the story out loud, stop at each blank, say the category, and have students read their words silently (or suggest when they think their word fits well) to create unique stories.

- Using any combination of words, drawing, and verbal storytelling, students can create stories that involve choices and take turns leading each other through what they've created.

Grades 3–5

- A story with even a few choices can get complicated very quickly. Choose a framework that will work with your students and have them sketch out possible plot paths on a planning sheet before they start to write.

- Your class can work together to create a huge story tree. Read your students the start of a story that ends in three or four choices. Those who choose each branch form a group and write that version of the story. They can include another set of choices, then split into smaller groups and continue writing. Have students add their pieces of the story to a large tree on the wall or board.

Grades 6–12

- Students can create how-to guides for each other based on academic topics or topics they are particularly interested in (how to be a social media star, how to make it to the NBA, how to watch or make a movie) and spend time working creatively and analytically.

- Find some examples of flowcharts that help with difficult or amusing questions or decisions. Students can create flowcharts for each other related to issues in school (Should I taste this chemical? What should I do when I'm stuck on a math problem?) or in life (Where should I go to college? How do I talk to someone I think is cute?).

Keep in Mind

When you are providing structure, students may try everything possible to break that structure or make it do something weird. Awesome. Let them do that.

Museum of Ideas

When we returned to in-person schooling after a COVID lockdown, Black History Month was just starting. Lockers weren't being used at the time, so I had every eighth grader create in a locker a miniature museum exhibit that related to Black history. I gave students a list of must-haves and can-haves and let their interests drive them from there. When the exhibits were ready, all the students in the school took turns by grade walking through the halls to explore and interact with the exhibits. Some teachers even created activities to enrich their museum visits. Find creative places in your school where students could set up similar exhibits about a topic of your choosing or topics driven by your students' curiosities.

> **More for You**
>
> The *New York Times* feature "What's Going On in This Graph?" can serve as a starting point for a data museum. Gapminder.org is another helpful tool for students to find, refine, or explore a topic.

Make It Real

Grades PK–2

- Each student builds a mini museum for a favorite book. Their exhibit can include the cover, a summary, main characters, and a review. (Give students a few categories with star ratings.) What else can students think of that represents the book or its audience?

- Give each student a "piece of history." These could be images, re-creations, or anything that represents an important person or place. For example, use a silver stamping of George Washington (a quarter). Students create a museum exhibit that features their piece of history.

Grades 3–5

- In addition to the "piece of history" suggestion at left, students can create exhibits about a "piece of science." Give them more freedom to design their exhibits and choose what information to include.

- Data exhibits give students a chance to be critical readers of numbers and graphs. Students can create data collection tools (see Data Collection strategy on page 35), or you could give them a wide range of interesting data sets or visual representations. Their exhibits can explain what the data shows (or misses) and demonstrate how to read the data.

Grades 6–12

- If the skill students are practicing (or you are assessing) is more important than the content of their exhibits, give them freedom to choose their own topic. This may lead to some interesting and complex projects, such as an investigation of primary sources from Nintendo's early days or a statistical analysis of an upcoming football season.

- Museum exhibits can facilitate communication and community building. Before they move on, your oldest students can create exhibits about memorable moments, teachers, or lessons learned.

Keep in Mind

If your exhibits will be in a public place, they shouldn't include anything that students absolutely need back or is valuable. Requiring objects or purchases from home can exclude some students, so plan your project in a way that ensures all students have access to what they need.

Mindful Movement

One of the tests I had to pass for my teacher licensure involved more math than I'd done in almost a decade. During the test, I looked to my left. The guy sitting there was opening his mouth and eyes as wide as he could, closing them, then doing it over and over. It looked as if he were silently screaming, falling asleep, and screaming again. After the test, I asked him what was going on, and he said it was a trick he did when he got tired during tests. Many years later, when I was teaching seventh grade, I had a student, a gymnast, who would sometimes do handstands against the wall during class discussions or direct instruction because it helped her think. Mindful movement isn't just yoga. There are lots of ways people can move that regulate their bodies and brains and help them work together.

More for You

Create an Emotion-Rich Classroom by Lindsay N. Giroux

Make It Real

Grades PK–2	Grades 3–5	Grades 6–12

• Teach your class one movement technique for each of three big feelings they may have:
 	
  • When you're angry, put a hand on your stomach and move it in and out with big breaths.
 	
  • When you're worried, shake your hands, shake your feet, then shake your body.
 	
  • When you're sleepy, touch three points in the room, then go back to your starting spot.
 	
• Practice your movements so students feel comfortable using them when they need to.
	• Teach a few movement sets that your class uses when students are switching disciplines or activities—enough to provide variety, but not so many that the routine feels random. For example, at a transition, you may call out, "Sunflower!" and the class knows to stand and touch their toes, then slowly rise up and reach their hands toward the sky. Later in the day, you might call out, "Drill time!" and students bounce imaginary balls in each hand five times, then take five imaginary shots at a hoop you make with your arms.	• You may worry that secondary students won't want to do any silly movements. In my experience, older kids love to be silly, move around, and take breaks just as much as younger kids do.
		
		• Encourage older students to find their own best ways to regulate. For my gymnast student, it was doing handstands if she'd been sitting still too long. For others, it might be fidgets. (I liked having chenille stems, or pipe cleaners, around for days I knew I'd be asking for a lot of listening.) When students find what works for them—not just what's fun for them—they acquire tools they can use long after your year together.

Keep in Mind

A student may feel uncomfortable participating in movement for any number of reasons. Work with the student to find their own strategy without shaming them.

Critical Thinking with Scissors

Deconstruction is a critical and difficult component of analysis. Whether you and your students are taking apart a new and difficult concept, an important passage, or a visual text, you can make the abstract a lot more concrete with some scissors and glue. Hand each student a copy of the text and a larger blank sheet of paper and instruct them to cut the original into its building blocks. Next, have them reimagine the text by placing its pieces on the blank page in a way that shows how they understand it. They could make a flowchart, place ideas in groups, or use some other creative approach to show the meanings they found.

More for You

Open Access at the Met (metmuseum.org/about-the-met/policies-and-documents/open-access); Open Access at the Art Institute of Chicago (artic.edu/open-access/open-access-images); *Get the Picture: Visual Literacy in Content-Area Instruction* by Marva Cappello and Nancy Walker

Make It Real

Grades PK–2

- Have students create pictorial charts for letter sounds, counting, or emotions. Give students many images to choose from by printing out emoji lists, royalty-free stock images, and/or images from books and curriculum in your classroom and library.

- Using images from a story you just read or from a variety of well-known stories and fairy tales, challenge students to create new stories that match the original(s) in some important way.

Grades 3–5

- When you're studying information that's organized in a specific way, such as a plot, a time line of events, the class of mammals, or chemical elements, have students cut the pieces apart and reorganize them in a new way, labeling and explaining their new groupings.

- Enlarge an important chunk of text from what you are studying and give copies to your students. Have each student cut out key words and phrases and present them in a way that shows tone, bias, or meaning, or links to other events and ideas.

Grades 6–12

- Use this strategy to practice critical analysis using artworks with lots of subtext and visual metaphor. Have each student create a visual using pieces of the original to show what they think the painting means. There is no right answer.

- Have students cut printouts of multiple paintings into small squares. (You can find thousands of free, downloadable, public-domain artworks through the Open Access programs of many museums.) Invite them to create their own visuals using those pieces plus their own writing or drawing to represent a concept, equation, event, or argument.

Keep in Mind

Circulate around the room, asking students what they are trying to show in the images they are creating and encouraging them to discuss this with each other. Talking through their ideas can help them expand on their work.

Blackout Poem or Message

Give each student a copy of one page of writing from a book or other text. Invite students to black out some of the text so the remaining words and phrases create a poem or message. This can be a fun and engaging way to have students explore texts. When taken a step further to focus specifically on tone, bias, voice, symbolism, evidence, or another point of study, this strategy can help students think both critically and creatively.

More for You

50 Strategies for Motivating Reluctant Readers by Heidi Crumrine

Make It Real

Grades PK–2	Grades 3–5	Grades 6–12
• Print just the words from a favorite story on one page, then have students color, cut, arrange, and glue them onto a large paper and illustrate with their own original drawings. • Give each student a sheet with a large list of words (or a story) on it. Have students search for words that have specific phonemes, or all nouns or verbs, or whatever you like, then draw and color around those words.	• Blackout art can help students show the main idea of a nonfiction text. Provide students with a text-only copy of nonfiction selection from current reading. Have students black out words in a way that leaves the most important words and phrases, conveys the main idea, and demonstrates understanding. • When you're studying tone, give students texts with neutral or opposite tones and see if they can make blackout poetry that conveys contrasting tones.	• Give students news stories, opinion articles, or primary source documents and have them use blackout to show things like bias, main idea, evidence, and so on. Have students design their own systems of colors and images to annotate a text. • When you're investigating a particularly complex text, give students a chance to explore and experiment with meaning by doing blackout poems.

Keep in Mind

You can find excellent examples of this strategy online. Before students start, show them many ways to do this well. This will help them think bigger about their own projects.

Vote with Your Feet

You've likely experienced this strategy in a professional development session. The presenter asks a question with multiple answers; various places in the room represent the answers. Each participant walks to the answer they choose. This strategy can help you get students out of their seats. You can either insist students make a binary choice or allow answers on a spectrum for questions that need more nuance.

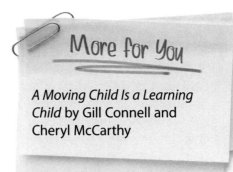

More for You

A Moving Child Is a Learning Child by Gill Connell and Cheryl McCarthy

Make It Real

Grades PK–2	Grades 3–5	Grades 6–12
• To activate student brains at the start of the day or after lunch, give students a series of quick yes-no questions and have them answer by moving to one side of the room or the other. Students can take turns asking their own questions too. • For a quick engagement check and movement break during a story, pause and ask students if they agree or disagree with the actions or reactions of a character. Give students a chance to explain why before gathering them again and continuing the story.	• Ask students to place themselves on a spectrum between agree and disagree, right and wrong, important and unimportant. Present them with various questions, statements, or scenarios. For example, if you're asking them to agree or disagree, you might say, "Pizza is delicious!" • Help students practice estimating. For example, ask, "How many penguins are in this picture? This wall represents one; that wall is one hundred. Stand between them where you think is right." • Form quick discussion groups. For example, say, "If your favorite character is Stanley, walk over there. If it's Zero, stand over here."	• Have students hypothesize about the results of an experience or form arguments based on a text or event, then gather with like-minded classmates. They must come up with strong evidence to support their claim and see if they can get anyone else to join their team. • Activate prior knowledge and do a quick preassessment by asking students to position themselves between "never heard of it" and "could teach it." One at a time, call out different names, concepts, or keywords from a new unit, giving students time to switch to a new spot between words.

Keep in Mind

This strategy works well for starting discs and sharing opinions, but avoid using it for questions with right and wrong answers—you don't want to publicly shame students standing in the wrong-answer spot. Also be careful not to ask questions that may be uncomfortable for some students, such as questions about family structure or other personal topics.

Build Knowledge from Stuff

Wouldn't it be nice if all brains worked and all students learned the same way? Well, it'd be nice because it would make teaching a lot easier, but decidedly not-nice because it would eliminate one of the coolest things about human brains: they're so different. If you go through my old math notebooks, you'll see lots of random doodles that look like nonsense. I often doodled to make sense of an idea. I tried to visualize ideas without using numbers. For many students, the act of translating information into new forms, especially physical representations, helps them synthesize and solidify learning about a concept (Rau 2017). The more choices they have about those physical representations, the more active and creative the exercise becomes.

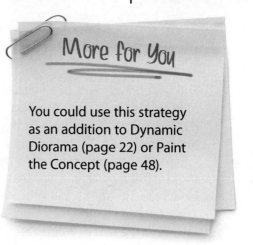

More for You

You could use this strategy as an addition to Dynamic Diorama (page 22) or Paint the Concept (page 48).

Make It Real

Grades PK–2	Grades 3–5	Grades 6–12
• Have students use manipulatives to practice counting or to represent addition or subtraction problems. • Using a light source and different-size balls or blocks, students can create a small individual or a large class-size representation of the solar system to show how day and night work or to visualize an upcoming eclipse.	• With chenille stems (pipe cleaners), paper, tape, and other craft materials, students can create representations of how measurement units relate to one another (how many centimeters in a meter, how many quarts in a gallon, and so forth). • Have students build and present models of the systems and cycles that make up the world around them, such as the water cycle, sunlight and photosynthesis, or even economic and education systems.	• As students encounter more and more abstract math, give them blocks, string, and other manipulatives to build formulas and equations. This can help get them investigating and discussing the concepts behind the numbers. • When students are learning about various government or economic systems, place them in groups and give each group one system to represent in physical form. Have the groups take turns presenting and explaining their models to each other.

Keep in Mind

When you picture a maker space, you might imagine building materials, tools, and an open-flame forge. Sure, that would be wonderful in every classroom, but you don't need to go all out to give students space to build. I don't know how many pipe cleaners (aka chenille stems) are used every year to clean pipes, but I'll bet a huge number of them are used for creating and learning. I'm thankful they are still cheap and readily available for students to make stuff with.

Map Your World

The key components of a map are a title, a key or legend, and indicators of scale and direction. Those components can show not just where a place is, but who might live there, what happens there, how people or things or weather move through the place, and where physical barriers and human boundaries are. Maps can tell the story of a place in a way that words cannot. For this strategy, have students start small with a map of your classroom or school. Then they can widen their view, perhaps to describe their routes to school or the places where they live. A map can zoom way in to a place of particular importance to students. A single map can also have different layers and legends to show many aspects of a place.

More for You

Many fascinating local mapping resources exist. I appreciate the Mapping Prejudice project from the University of Minnesota (mappingprejudice.umn.edu). What mapping projects can you find near you?

Make It Real

Grades PK–2	Grades 3–5	Grades 6–12
• Give each student a blank map of your school building, the local area, or the region and have them create their own legend and add symbols to the map by drawing or using stickers. Where is there food? Where can they play? What else is around? • At the beginning of the year, send students in small groups (with an adult) out into the school with a map that leads to a few key points (bathroom, front office, gym, health room). Have them use the map to find places and get passport stamps from the staff there.	• School maps offer a way to talk with students about how they experience your building. What landmarks do students add to the school map? Where would they draw lines between grade levels? Which spaces are kid or adult spaces? Where do they go for help and what places do they avoid ("here be dragons")? • Get outdoors and walk the neighborhood with your students, bringing only paper, rulers, clipboards, and pencils. Each student can record their own map of what they see, or students can work in groups devoted to different types of maps (nature, buildings, transportation, and so forth).	• Give students a couple of days of introduction to mapmaking, then turn them loose on creating their own multi-map projects that show the world they live in. The results are sure to be astounding, creative, and powerful. Students may map relationships, cultures, access to services, personal and family histories, and more. Conversations started while presenting those maps can continue all year long.

Keep in Mind

Any activity that involves drawing can be nerve-racking for some students, especially those who are self-conscious about how their drawings look or who would rather just trace something. Try to help students focus on the ideas and the thinking they are representing, not on creating a flawless final product.

Picture Detectives

This strategy works well as a lesson warm-up to activate prior knowledge, raise questions and curiosity about a topic, and work on skills such as observation and evidence gathering. I learned it through the nonprofit Visual Thinking Strategies (vtshome.org), who offer all sorts of helpful resources and trainings. The basic idea is to put any interesting image in front of students and ask them what's going on in it, what they see that makes them answer as they do, and what more they can find. Make sure students understand that there are no right or wrong answers and that different interpretations are welcome. Students may build on each other's ideas but should not try to prove each other wrong. (Adapted with permission.)

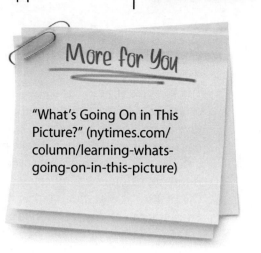

More for You

"What's Going On in This Picture?" (nytimes.com/column/learning-whats-going-on-in-this-picture)

Make It Real

Grades PK–2	Grades 3–5	Grades 6–12
• Use pictures, paintings, or sketches related to content or themes you are studying to reinforce learning. Give students space to answer and ask questions about what they see. • Examine still frames from popular movies to help students practice looking for and discussing details.	• Start with a small piece of an image, either cropped or zoomed in, then slowly reveal more and more, and ask, "What's going on *now*?" • To spark a lively conversation, place images or texts from different perspectives next to each other, or show one and then the other. For example, juxtapose photos of the real newspaper headlines "Dewey Defeats Truman" and "Truman Elected President," or show someone taking a selfie and the selfie itself.	• Use this strategy as a regular warm-up. Once students are accustomed to examining pictures closely, try using text (poems, speeches, school rules), pieces of video or music, or news stories. • Activate prior knowledge at the beginning of a lesson by choosing a rich image related to what you're studying.

Keep in Mind

Reinforce that no suggestion is bad or wrong, as long as it is backed by evidence. Ask, "What do you see that makes you say that?" and allow multiple readings of the same image. Take care when using an image that could spur a conversation about culture, identity, or trauma, and ensure that these are treated with full respect.

Follow Your Path

Think of this strategy as a flowchart in real life. For example, you could use this strategy to help students learn to identify insects. You could give a student at the starting station a picture of an insect and ask if it has wings. If it does, the student moves to the station on the left, and if it doesn't, they move to the station on the right. At the second station is the next step of identification. If students follow the path correctly, the picture at their final station should match the picture in their hand. Students can also work backward from a group of final stations and create their own questions and stations to classify the final items. They can then walk forward through the stations to test their work.

More for You

50 Strategies for Teaching STEAM Skills by Kara Ball has lots of great ideas for making active, thought-provoking math and science lessons.

Make It Real

Grades PK–2

- Make important lessons feel more real and more comfortable by setting up a path for students to follow in an emergency (if they smell smoke at night), through class procedures (when they have a question), or in social situations (if they have a disagreement with a classmate).

- Use an unexpected combination of pictures that show varying numbers and features to help students practice counting. Give each student a picture of a funny monster, a spaceship, or different groups of kittens (but only those three options) and set up stations based on the number of eyes, noses, legs, wings, wheels, or whatever.

Grades 3–5

- Pair this activity with Scavenger Hunts (page 43) and have students find examples of a specific aspect of local ecology (insects, trees, flowers, or leaves). Then come back to the classroom and set up paths to identify those items. Make sure to include a path for something that isn't listed in your scavenger hunt, and provide a way to research more broadly.

Grades 6–12

- Create a flowchart that illustrates why order of operations is important. Give students an equation with multiple steps, then have them try paths that do those steps in different orders to find the result for each path. Afterward, discuss where students struggled and what those different answers could mean. (For example: if you were being paid a certain amount every time someone clicked on an ad online, but had to give a certain amount if they skipped it, what happens when you switch the order of operations when calculating? What happens in the real world if you don't get the equation right?)

Keep in Mind

This strategy can involve a lot of setup if you try to create all the components yourself. Look for flowcharts online or in your class materials, think of ways students can contribute, and be ready for the activity to not work quite right the first time.

50 Strategies for Learning without Screens—152568

Frayer Models

Developed by Dorothy Frayer and her colleagues in 1969 at the University of Wisconsin (Go Badgers!), a Frayer model is a deceptively simple tool for tackling complex ideas. It helps students define or clarify the meaning of vocabulary words. The Frayer model is a square divided into four smaller squares. Starting at the top left square and working clockwise, the boxes are labeled "examples," "nonexamples," "nonessential characteristics," and "essential characteristics." No matter what a student suggests, it should fit somewhere in this model. Frayer models work well in small groups because they spark rich discussion about where a specific word should go. For example, if the concept you are defining is "breakfast," where does "pizza" go? How about "morning"?

More for You

Connecting Content and Language for English Language Learners by Eugenia Mora-Flores

Breakfast
(sample Frayer model from one of my classes)

Examples	**Nonexamples**
Eggs	A Ferrari
Cereal	Sushi
Bacon	Enchiladas
Breakfast tacos	The moon
Ful	Hot pizza*
Cold pizza*	Just coffee
Essential Characteristics	**Nonessential Characteristics**
Food	Warm
First meal of the day*	In the morning

*These items were the most debated during the class. That debate helped shape *why* something was or wasn't breakfast.

(continued)

Make It Real

Grades PK–2	Grades 3–5	Grades 6–12
• Students can categorize using images or stickers with a Frayer model. You will likely want to find simpler, more kid-friendly wording. Start with just two categories ("is" and "is not") before expanding to four.	• Students can build their own Frayer models and use them to define central terms, then go through a list of possibilities and see where they would fit. (For example: create a model of what makes a mammal and go through a list of creatures to see if the model works, or create models for fiction versus nonfiction and place a series of books.)	• I love the discussions and the thinking that Frayer models inspire around seemingly simple concepts. Starting simple is also important so that students have mastered the tool when they move on to defining more complex ideas. (I've seen or used Frayer models to create class definitions of terms such as *racism*, *intelligence*, *art*, and *American*.)
• A prefilled Frayer model of "examples," "not examples," "must have," and "might have" can help students categorize foods, animals, plants, and other items.	• When you introduce a new concept in class, create a Frayer model together to gauge your students' current understanding. Rebuilding that same Frayer definition from scratch at the end of the unit as a review will give you data on how students' thinking evolved over the lesson or unit.	• Using a Frayer model to create class definitions can open a conversation about why mutual understanding of a word is important before discussions and debates and can show how any given definition of a word is not necessarily the "right" one.

Keep in Mind

Starting with simple, low-stakes examples is fun, but it's also a time when you need to be vigilant about helping students use the tool correctly.

Data Collection

Students in my classroom know that I love when they express their opinions. They also know that I will almost always follow up by asking, "What makes you think that?" I want my students to be in the habit of bringing data to the table whenever possible. I should be clear that I am using the broadest possible definition of *data*. Data means numbers, measurements, and results, yes—and it also includes narratives, quotes, analysis, and observations. Data can look different depending on what you're trying to prove and how you're trying to prove it. The key is building the skills to gather data, assess it for quality and relevance, and share it effectively. For any discussion involving data, I suggest using some version of these three questions:

More for You

Street Data by Shane Safir and Jamila Dugan

- How do we know this?
- What is missing?
- What else can we find?

Make It Real

Grades PK–2	Grades 3–5	Grades 6–12
• Data collection fits well with the way young students are working to make sense of the world. Simple questions ("Which pole is farther away?") can turn into lessons when you ask follow-up questions ("How can we tell? How could we measure? Let's try a few ways and see what we learn.").	• Practice hypothesis, observation, and analysis by having students develop a simple hypothesis based on something at school. (For example: "90 percent of kindergartners will wave back if you wave at them in the hallway.") Then have students collect data and form a conclusion or a question for further study.	• Ask students to find a poll, survey, or statistic they are curious about, then investigate the methodology of the survey and identify how changes in method may affect the results. What if people answered on a scale rather than yes or no? What if the question were phrased differently?
• Practice counting, categorizing, and estimating by asking students to guess how many flowers they can find outside or how many books of each color are in the library. Then have them use a data collection sheet to count and see how close they got.	• When studying tone, perspective, or other aspects of literature, have students create a data set of words used within a page or two of a text. Provide categories or have students come up with their own.	• Assign students various metrics to track while watching a few minutes of a sport (number of passes, attempts, misses, or fouls) or while reading a passage (number of verbs, adjectives, or emotion words). What conclusions could they draw from the data?

Keep in Mind

The world is home to a wide variety of value systems. Some data may be more or less trustworthy depending on how it was gathered, who is sharing it, or who is listening. Even a large amount of great data does not tell a full story.

Advertise Your Knowledge

Young people are constant targets of advertising, and therefore can be insightful critics of advertising strategies. Put their experience and knowledge to use by having students make their own advertisements for things they have learned. It can be helpful and illuminating to give students a chance to track the advertisements they see in a given period (on the ride to school, during an hour of television, or in ten minutes on social media) and discuss what works and what doesn't before they make their own advertisements.

More for You

Generation Like (pbs.org/ wgbh/frontline/documentary/ generation-like)

Make It Real

Grades PK–2

- Have students work together on posters or other types of ads that advertise one aspect of something they are learning. Challenge students to creatively express their learning with just a simple phrase, a logo or picture, and a title.

- Show students examples of three advertisements directed at people their age. Invite them to identify how each ad is selling something and how it makes them feel. Next, have them make an ad for something free that they like to do.

Grades 3–5

- While studying a specific time period or branch of science or math, have students make ads for important inventions and ideas of the time. Showing students advertisements from that time, if possible, can help unlock their creativity—as can inviting them to create modern ads for historic products.

- Ask students to identify one advertisement they've seen while watching videos, going to school, or playing games. In groups, have students identify the ad's message and how it conveys that message. Next, have students make positive ads promoting community or kindness in the school.

Grades 6–12

- Have students create an advertising campaign related to your content. The campaign can include print ads, commercials, sponsorship ideas, and/or scripts for influencer posts on social media.

- At home, have students track all the advertisements they see in a certain time period while they're using social media or watching videos online. Have them write all the brands they spotted on the board or on a few pieces of chart paper. After discussing techniques, students can design an anti-advertising or wellness campaign.

Keep in Mind

Making their own advertisements intended to appeal to others can help students be aware of how they are targeted to feel or think a certain way by real-world advertisements. Picture Detectives (page 31) and Critical Thinking with Scissors (page 26) are also strategies for analyzing ads.

Crayon Quiz

This strategy provides all the things that are most important about any short comprehension quiz. It allows students to reflect on the work they've done that week, make sure they understand key concepts and ideas, and spend some time talking about it with each other. A crayon quiz is perfect for a Friday or anytime the brains and bodies in the room need a little break but you still want to do something meaningful. The key components are as follows: minimal instructions, a few big sheets of paper, and a whole bunch of crayons.

More for You

Get the Picture: Visual Literacy in Content-Area Instruction by Marva Cappello and Nancy Walker

Make It Real

Grades PK–2

- Have students work alone or together to draw scenes from a book you've read as a class.

- Choose two emotions from a story and have your students work together to draw and write pictures and words that capture those emotions.

Grades 3–5

- Using a shared text, have a group of students work around a single large sheet of paper. Give them a list of must-have images, including characters, places, and what they feel is the most important part of the story, and have them include quotes from the story that helped them picture those things.

- Rather than quiz students on what you think they should know, ask them to tell you everything they know or remember about a topic or lesson. Encourage them to use their crayons to share visuals and words that represent their learning.

Grades 6–12

- On the board, write a list of things each group must share from the reading from that week, such as important scenes, characters, and plot points. Give each group a certain number of elements they must contribute. For example: three quotes, three drawn images, and two symbols.

- Instruct students to create their own combination of elements that summarize their learning of a specific topic or unit.

Keep in Mind

It may take a few tries before students feel comfortable sharing their drawings. It can help to underscore that the goal is to show thinking, not to create a finished art piece.

Group Poems

Writing poetry can sometimes feel scary to students because it makes them feel vulnerable. By working in groups, students can practice the form, imagery, and language elements of poetic writing while having fun together and taking the pressure off individuals. Place students into small groups. Have each group sit in a circle and give a sheet of paper and a pen to each student. Each student starts by writing a line on their paper and then passing it to the student on their left. Add a little fun and chaos by having each student fold over their line before passing to the next student so each student is writing without context. After a set amount of time or number of lines, have students read the poems in their hands out loud to the class.

More for You

What the Science of Reading Says: Literacy Strategies for Early Childhood by Jodene L. Smith; *Literacy Strategies for Grades 1–2* by Erica Bowers; *What the Science of Reading Says: Literacy Strategies for Grades 3–5* by Laura Keisler; and *What the Science of Reading Says: Literacy Strategies for Secondary Grades* by Laura Keisler

Make It Real

Grades PK–2	Grades 3–5	Grades 6–12
• Group poems can help students practice rhyming. Read the first line of a rhyming couplet and have students make suggestions for the second line of the couplet.	• Give middle-grade students a list of rhyming words to use, a starting line or word, or a content-related topic to help keep the poems from becoming a series of nonsense lines or fart jokes.	• After reading a particular poet or type of poem, invite each group of students to write a poem together in the same style.
• Groups or individuals can make up lines back and forth with a series of letter sounds. (For example: the first line uses as many "ah" words as they can think of, the second uses "be" words, and so on.)	• Provide a list of famous first and last lines of poetry and have each group choose one first and one last line. Challenge each group to write a poem that connects the first and last lines in a way that makes sense.	• Group poems are a fun way to let students review and explore ideas on any topic. Ask students to rewrite elements of biology or geometry as poetically as possible—the more over-the-top, the better!
• Place students into groups and give each group a poem missing the word at the end of each line and a supply of cut-out words that rhyme in pairs. Have groups finish their poems together using the words provided.		

Keep in Mind

Writing with other people can feel challenging for some students. If students are reading each other's rough work, remind them not to comment on spelling or handwriting.

Human Teleprompter

Turn a class discussion or debate into a fun, dynamic activity. With groups of students representing two or more sides of a discussion, have one person from each group assume the role of speaker, while others serve as the "teleprompter." Teleprompters feed their speakers pros and cons, arguments and responses, and any other statements they might need. Teleprompters can use sheets of paper, sticky notes, whiteboards, or whatever else works to hand off messages to their speakers. This strategy helps students speak publicly while spreading out the responsibility for what is said, and it lets students who don't want to speak still have their ideas represented in the room.

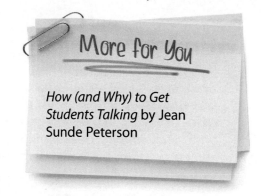

More for You

How (and Why) to Get Students Talking by Jean Sunde Peterson

Make It Real

Grades PK–2	Grades 3–5	Grades 6–12
• Play a quiz game in which students take different roles as contestants, runners, and researchers. Place students into groups of at least three. Researchers hand or whisper the answer to a runner, who hands or whispers it to the contestant. • A few students act out a scene in which each character is controlled by a group of classmates. The groups tells their characters what to say and how to act.	• Hold a debate around an issue you are studying (whether Pluto is a planet, what the voting age should be, a new amendment to the Bill of Rights). Groups on each side of the debate have access to important texts and other research. Teleprompters feed their debaters facts and quotes for each new round. • Host debates and discussions surrounding ideas important to students to help them think critically about complex issues—for example, the right age to get a smartphone, how many hours the school day should last, or something else the students propose. Halfway through the debate, have students switch sides in the argument.	• Have the speaking students take the role of important historical or scientific figures. They don't even need to be people; one student could speak as alternating current (AC) electricity and another could be direct current (DC); one student could be classic novels and another could be modern young adult fiction. Teleprompters feed their speakers arguments, evidence, and quotes. • Have the researchers and writers prepare responses and counterarguments for what they feel the opposing side's best arguments will be, so they are ready to hand them to the speaker mid-debate. For arguments they don't predict, they will need to write fast or let the speaker try to handle it on their own.

Keep in Mind

A student may be told to say something they do not agree with. If the student doesn't want to make such a statement, another student can tag in to make the point or can submit it to you.

Collaborative Reading

Reading aloud is a valuable practice, especially for challenging texts. Give each student their own copy of a challenging text with plenty of space to write in and have them read the text aloud together multiple times, with different goals during each reading. In the end, each student will have a text that illustrates the importance of reading closely and of collaborating. Tell students to follow these steps:

More for You

Letters of Note (lettersofnote. com); *Using Primary Sources in the Classroom, Second Edition* by Kathleen Vest

1. Read aloud as a group, marking words you don't know with a question mark.

2. Write definitions for the marked terms in your own words, using context clues and a dictionary.

3. Reread the text aloud together, underlining words and phrases that feel important.

4. Read aloud together again, circling phrases that connect to something in your life or your learning.

5. Reread the text out loud a final time, highlighting passages that feel powerful or beautiful.

Make It Real

Grades PK–2	Grades 3–5	Grades 6–12
• Use a text that's challenging but familiar to students, such as the words to a popular song or story or to the national anthem. • If students need help with step two, ask them to show you their efforts to figure out the meanings of words before giving them definitions.	• As students are learning to access subtext, metaphor, and other figurative language, give them as large a sheet as you can print with a poem, then have them work together to read the poem many times while highlighting (or drawing) different kinds of figurative descriptions. • Assign roles (a researcher, a linguist who focuses on language and definitions, an analyst who works on connections within the text, a recorder who writes and keeps notes) to members of the group. These roles can rotate with every new reading or can stay stable.	• This is a particularly effective strategy for complex texts—especially important primary source documents you want students to investigate closely. • See page 70 for a full secondary lesson using Martin Luther King Jr.'s "Letter from Birmingham Jail." (Amanda Gorman's poem "The Hill We Climb" would work well for this lesson too.)

Keep in Mind

Be especially thoughtful with your choice of text. Rich texts will help students understand the importance of repeated, thoughtful readings.

You Need a Protocol

It's not usually hard to get students talking, but it can be a challenge to make a discussion productive. One key to good conversations, especially when there are disagreements, is to first set a protocol, or a set of rules, for the discussions. Rehearse the protocol before you start a discussion. There are a lot of great conversation protocols out there; choose the one you like best. Emphasize to students that in all conversations, the goal is to understand each other, not to "win."

More for You

Courageous Conversations About Race, Third Edition by Glenn E. Singleton

Make It Real

Grades PK–2

- Early elementary students are often capable of complex thoughts but may struggle to communicate them effectively. Use feelings charts to describe emotions or physical or visual ways to express agreement or disagreement, such as a sticker vote placed along a spectrum of agreement.

- Use sentence stems such as "I believe," "I think," or "What I see is" to help students focus their thoughts and how they are sharing.

- Develop and practice nonverbal ways to show appreciation or support for an idea.

Grades 3–5

- Truly brilliant conversations can come about over shared texts or ideas by using structured discussion protocols with clear goals, such as Socratic Seminars.

- Guiding questions, such as "What did you learn from that student's statement?" or "Does anyone have a different idea?," can help frame a classroom conversation away from right versus wrong and toward learning from and understanding each other.

Grades 6–12

- Before diving into challenging conversations, practice your protocol with low-stakes, high-engagement discussions, such as "What defines breakfast?" or "Is a hot dog a sandwich?"

- For secondary students, I love the Courageous Conversation protocol from the Pacific Educational Group. I used this protocol as my classroom rules.

Keep in Mind

There are countless protocols for classroom discussions. Find one that makes sense for you, your style, and your students. It will not go perfectly at first, but time spent reinforcing a place for productive, positive conversations will pay dividends all year.

Timed Talks

I'm more comfortable speaking in front of a few hundred people than I am ordering a pizza over the phone, but I understand public speaking consistently ranks near the top on surveys of greatest fears. Still, it's one of those things that's important to learn to do well. Solo talks in front of the class can help your students get to know each other while activating background knowledge around a topic. Structure and limits can help everyone feel a little more comfortable about speaking to an audience. Students who are truly anxious about speaking in front of their classmates could make videos or podcast recordings, or (one of my favorites, if you can manage it) they could talk while walking around the building with you.

More for You

"How Every Child Can Thrive by Five," a TED talk by seven-year-old Molly Wright (ted.com/talks/molly_wright _how_every_child_can_ thrive_by_five)

Make It Real

Grades PK–2	Grades 3–5	Grades 6–12
• Ask students to talk about a time they were surprised, a story with an animal, or whatever topic fits your teaching. Timing the talks reassures timid students that they won't have to stand up there forever and keeps loquacious students from hogging the mic. • Give students some structure and planning time even though the talks are short and casual. Each student can plan by writing or drawing a beginning, middle, and end to their talk. Showing a tangible object from home or the classroom would be helpful as well.	• A timed talk can be presented in character from the point of view of an ancestor, historical figure, or fictional character, as a way to humanize content students are learning. A picture, object, or audio recording related to the topic can help focus the talk. • Middle-grade students can benefit from identifying, researching, and discussing their passions. This approach gives them a way to bring more of themselves into the classroom, learn about each other, and practice planning and writing speeches with topics they are comfortable talking about.	• Students can start with a simple speech format (introduction, body, conclusion), then add other public speaking tools such as personal anecdotes, memorable quotes, evidence, visuals, emotional appeals, humor, and calls to action. • Timed talks can inspire students to dig deeper into curriculum or to look outside the classroom at how what they're learning connects to the wider world. They can also encourage students to dream big, describe the perfect school, propose a solution to a complex problem, imagine an invention, or identify an aspiration.

Keep in Mind

Learning to listen is even more important than learning to speak effectively. Review expectations and goals for an actively listening and supportive audience.

Scavenger Hunts

One of my favorite memories of childhood is the day when my family visited the National Zoo in Washington, DC, and my two older cousins made a scavenger hunt for the younger kids to help us explore the grounds and stay busy. A scavenger hunt helps kids see the world in new ways, notice details they might otherwise ignore, look for patterns, and think collaboratively to solve puzzles and accomplish a shared goal. Scavenger hunts can be used with just about any topic and across disciplines.

More for You

The Playful Classroom by Jed Dearybury and Julie Jones

Make It Real

Grades PK–2	Grades 3–5	Grades 6–12
• In a large space such as a playground, gym, or assembly area, students can search for hidden shapes, letters, or numbers in the world and draw what they see. • When practicing specific word sounds, students can look around for things in the world whose names have that sound. • Students can also search the world around them for things related to science concepts. For example, how many things can students find that feed their bodies in different ways? Or that plants or insects could use?	• A list of fractions, descriptive words, or science concepts can make for an interesting scavenger hunt. For example, what can students find and draw or describe that shows the concept $\frac{3}{5}$? • A scavenger hunt through the neighborhood of your school (or on a field trip bus ride) allows students to use the world around them to look for the history of the place and people; ways that industry, technology, and population have changed the area; or how geography and people interact.	• For a homeroom or advisory activity, teachers across a grade level can all add their own "puzzle" clues to a scavenger hunt using pieces of their curriculum. Students could stay in their homeroom but access ideas from around the school to complete the hunt. Alternately, the clues could be with those subject-area teachers, and when students give a correct answer, the teacher gives out the next clue, leading the group to a place. • Take students on a scavenger hunt to identify various engineering problems and their solutions (for example, rain gutters in streets to prevent flooding, traffic lights to prevent crashes).

Keep in Mind

The goal of this strategy is to get students thinking about the world in new ways. When developing your scavenger hunt, make sure the clues or list items you supply require some creative and critical thinking to solve and find.

Do You Want to Build a Snowman?

More for You

The Gift of Playful Learning by Nadia Kenisha Bynoe and Angelique Thompson

Advisory always hit my teaching team like an emergency, even though it happened every week at the same time. We would gather around a table trying to plan a meaningful twenty-minute activity five minutes before it was supposed to start. One day, after our first big snow of the winter, our science teacher suggested we hold a snow-building competition. Indoors. Students grabbed recycling bins and filled them outdoors and brought them to the science room that had a floor drain. They worked in pairs and groups to build snow sculptures as quickly as possible. It was a beautiful disaster. It was the most fun anyone involved ever had in advisory and was by far the worst idea I've ever seen done well. Do it. I dare you. Or do something different but equally silly and messy and fun. Great learning often comes from doing big dumb things.

Make It Real

Grades PK–2

- You've probably done finger painting with your students at some point, but how about foot painting? Give families a heads-up about the messy day, have some cling wrap handy to cover up clothing, and find a space to lay down lots of paper. Then, encourage your students to make some art by dipping their feet in paint and walking around on the paper.

- Are there any nature areas near your school? What can students create with natural items they find on the ground? What kinds of art or construction do students create when they get time to collect stuff and make it into other stuff?

Grades 3–5

- You know that tub in your classroom or the supply closet full of broken old crayons? Have students take the paper labels off those crayons and glue the crayons onto paper, lay them in a frame of some kind, or make crayon shavings. Then come around with a hair dryer or an iron to melt the crayons and see what art they create.

- On warm days, a lot of fun can be had making colored water into ice cubes and heading outside with some blank paper and plastic gloves.

Grades 6–12

- There will need to be strict rules around snowballs being thrown. (And if you are anything like every secondary teacher I've ever known, those rules are mostly to keep *you* from throwing snowballs inappropriately.)

- Listen, listen, listen. Your students will have much better (worse?) ideas than you will, and giving them a chance to drive your activities will help them feel engaged and empowered.

Keep in Mind

You know your school culture, your community, and your bosses better than I do. Don't get fired.

Escape Room

Escape rooms encourage active learning and teamwork, so they're an excellent way to promote collaborative thinking. Quick searches online can reveal lots of support for setting up an escape room—and plenty of free ones. After you've created or completed one escape room (which is really just a series of puzzles connected by a story), the real fun comes in having students create escape rooms for each other.

More for You

This strategy works well paired with other imagination-rich strategies like Role-Playing (page 59) and Scavenger Hunts (page 43).

Make It Real

Grades PK–2	Grades 3–5	Grades 6–12
• Young students may struggle to come up with specific puzzles that make sense to anyone but themselves, but they are great at coming up with stories that connect puzzles. On conference or open house nights, students can walk their families through the escape room they made as a class. • Play up the theatrical aspect of the escape room. You aren't standing in a classroom, you're in a spaceship that needs repairs or inside the mind of someone who forgot how to handle their feelings. If the students all work together, they can save the day!	• Given a basic setup for an escape room (maybe five parts that come together to make a key or a series of clues that lead one to the next), students can work in small groups to write their own stories and clues. Team up with another teacher and have them lead their students through what your students have created. • You can create puzzles in your escape room specific to a topic or time period you are studying in class. Each puzzle solved might reveal a piece of a larger image or a more challenging new puzzle. Different kinds of puzzles can tap into essential skills students have been learning all year.	• Given enough time and tools, older students can make their own props, physical puzzles, and clues. After running through one or two practice versions to get ideas, students can work on their escape room in advisory or homeroom over the course of a month or two. Or a class could do this as a final project. • Be sure to mix up the kinds of clues and puzzles students will interact with. To review math concepts, some clues can involve finding patterns, some might involve putting pieces of an equation back together so it makes sense, some could use the physical space, and some might require deductive reasoning.

Keep in Mind

Process is often more important than product. Your escape room may not be ready for a social media close-up, but that doesn't mean it won't be engaging, educational, and memorable. Be aware that common escape room narratives such as pretending to imprison or trap someone, defuse a bomb, or the like could be really triggering in a classroom setting.

Towers and Bridges and Stuff

You've likely done projects like this before—building towers out of noodles, making bridges out of straws, constructing egg drops and marble roller coasters. They're fun, they're often competitive, and they get students' brains going. For classrooms really struggling to close their laptops and put their phones away, these proven high-engagement activities can encourage creative thinking, collaboration, learning from failure, and joy. If you feel like your students have done and seen them all, just look a little harder. (See the book recommendation at right.)

More for You

50 Strategies for Teaching STEAM Skills by Kara Ball

Make It Real

Grades PK–2

- Marble mazes are fun and can be built by kids of all ages (with a little hot-glue help from an adult). Have each student draw a maze on a paper plate or shoebox, glue straws on the lines, and try to roll a large marble through the maze. Remind kids that marbles don't belong in bodies.

- More complex engineering can be done as a class. If you're making a bridge, show students three materials and have them guess how many blocks each material would hold. Then show students three bridge variations using the strongest material. After testing those, have them draw designs for a strong bridge using what they learned.

Grades 3–5

- Building a tower using only paper and tape can help groups of students plan and solve problems together. Give students chances to test pieces of their design, then adapt and rebuild. (Some versions of this activity involve scarcity as a challenge. For example, supply a very small amount of tape. But be aware that too much scarcity may limit students' creativity.)

- This strategy can help build community, but students may need some guidance on how to offer criticism, what to do when an idea doesn't work, and how to include all group members.

Grades 6–12

- Let older students experiment with real-world challenges. Is there a hallway with a traffic-flow problem? A need for more comfortable seating or ideas to make cleaning after lunch more fun for students? Making this a longer, more involved inquiry project and giving them room to research, explore, and experiment will be well worth the time.

- As you plan, make sure you have clear goals. Is this a community-building activity? Do you want students using math or science concepts? Is it important that students communicate and collaborate? Plan and proceed accordingly.

Keep in Mind

Some of the best learning happens after the first try fails and students have to go back and change their designs based on new information. Make sure you've allowed time for failing and trying again.

Sticky Linguists

Have you ever used a new slang word or texted an emoji to a younger person and done so slightly wrong? If so, then you already know that young people are accomplished linguists. Their grasp of the rules of language in their lives is often far more complex than they realize. Help them articulate what they know about the structure of language with this strategy. Have students work as a group to brainstorm words on any topic and write each word on a sticky note. Then challenge them to come up with their own categories for the words and explain their reasoning. Sit back and listen; you will hear some truly incredible insight and investigation into the parts of language. This strategy is perfect for exploring words around identity, activating background knowledge on a topic, or exploring parts of speech.

More for You

You Have Feelings All the Time
by Deborah Farmer Kris

Make It Real

Grades PK–2	Grades 3–5	Grades 6–12
• On a wall or on chart paper, create sections for different emotions. Have your students draw or write emotion-related pictures, symbols, or words on sticky notes. Then see how many ways students can think of to organize and reorganize the stickies.	• Display an interesting artwork or photo—related to a topic you are studying, if possible. Instruct students in small groups to brainstorm words they would use to describe the artwork or photo and write the words on sticky notes. Have students divide the stickies into categories of their own choosing or into parts of speech.	• Budding adolescent sociologists love to study and question the world around them. Ask them to brainstorm words that are used to describe young people, people from your region, or other aspects of identity (depending on the level of trust and safety the group feels with you and each other). This activity can help them see how language is used to build the world they live in.

Keep in Mind

The words themselves may be less important than what kinds of words they are. Group discussions about why they originally thought of so many specific kinds of words can illuminate strengths or blind spots in perception.

Paint the Concept

This strategy is simple to explain but can be challenging to execute. It asks students to turn a concrete representation of a concept into an abstract one. This can be done in many ways, but there's something wonderful about a roomful of students conveying an idea through watercolor or pastels. Have your students just spent a week on a challenging concept such as the water cycle, dividing fractions, or the types of government? Challenge them to create a visual of the concept using shapes and colors.

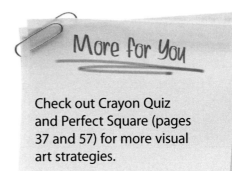

More for You

Check out Crayon Quiz and Perfect Square (pages 37 and 57) for more visual art strategies.

Make It Real

Grades PK–2	Grades 3–5	Grades 6–12
• Depending on the concept your students are working on, you might give them certain shapes or images they can color and glue on a new sheet of paper. • Divide a complex idea into parts. Have some students create images of one part, have other students create images of another part, and so on. Then place students in groups with each part represented and challenge each group to put the concept together.	• To encourage abstract thinking, put some limits on what students can paint. For example, if students are painting their understanding of a math concept, have them do so without using numbers. • Pair this strategy with another assignment. After students have researched, written, or presented, have them paint a version of whatever they just did.	• During the secondary grades, most core subjects move from concrete to abstract concepts. Give students a chance to absorb and reflect on some of those big ideas (such as variables, economic systems, subtext, causation, and so forth) by painting them. • Offer students a chance to reflect and gather their thoughts after a reading, discussion, or video by giving them each a small square of paper and pastels or crayons to express their reactions.

Keep in Mind

If your students have not done a lot of artistic work in class before, especially in an abstract or open way, it may take them a few attempts to get comfortable with it.

One-Minute Skit

Some of the strategies in this section involve exposing students to what is, for some, a very scary thing: a blank page. A one-minute skit is a fun way to have students review recent learning, make a well-constructed argument, or experiment with a concept—*without* having to write about it. Because the skit is short, it feels low-stakes and provides good practice for editing and clear, concise communication.

More for You

Build Reading Fluency: Practice and Performance with Reader's Theater and More, Second Edition by Timothy Rasinski and Chase Young

Make It Real

Grades PK–2	Grades 3–5	Grades 6–12
• The one-minute limit compels students to improvise short scenes instead of writing or otherwise planning them before performing. Students can write and revise afterward if they want to. • Students can act out math concepts or problems, classroom routines, emotions, or other ideas to move, work together, and explore. • Skits don't always need an audience. Splitting students among multiple "stage" areas means everyone can act at the same time.	• Giving students a variety of roles to choose from (director, actor, researcher, and so on) can ease planning. Give students stopwatches or timers to use as they rehearse so they can try to make their skits exactly one minute long. • Skits can help students engage with the ideas of people or places they are studying, and they can also be a fun way to show understanding of scientific phenomena or tackle complex problems from multiple angles.	• Before studying *Romeo and Juliet*, group students by act and have each group do a short skit summarizing the action in their act. They can perform for each other one at a time with some explanation, and then do the whole play in just a few minutes. A firm grasp on the plot points can help students focus on the language and characters while reading. • Short skits can be a starting point for tackling ethical or complex dilemmas in science or social studies. Groups of students can present their skits and facilitate class discussion afterward.

Keep in Mind

You may have students who are reluctant to perform in front of the class. Include them in writing and directing instead of performing.

The Languages in Our Lives

To foster curiosity about the machinations and complexities of language, this strategy challenges students to be researchers in their own world, defining and examining the languages, dialects, and code-switching happening around them all the time. The equation of this strategy is simple: take one reference or analysis tool (such as a dictionary or a phrase book), add a few pieces of a student's life, then invite them to study the languages in their lives like a sociologist. You could also use this strategy with traditions, behaviors, or advertising messages.

Make It Real

More for You

The Language and Life Project (languageandlife. org) offers documentaries, research, and examples of dialects spoken all over the United States and shows how to talk about language respectfully and academically.

Grades PK–2	Grades 3–5	Grades 6–12
• Provide a sheet with images of common items or concepts that can be named with different words. Challenge students to come up with as many words as they can to describe the items or bring the sheet home to ask family and community members.	• Assign this activity before a long break during which students are likely to see family or participate in community gatherings. Have students jot down words and phrases they hear in various settings or interview adults about common phrases or sayings they like.	• This can be a powerful lesson on how language changes depending on the situation or participants. You can work with students to create a recording template by asking what might be different in the ways people talk to each other and discussing how to notate those differences. Then have students take notes on language patterns in three different spaces.

Keep in Mind

In linguistics, there is no "right" or "wrong" way to speak. This strategy offers an opportunity to affirm the value of the languages and dialects spoken and heard by all your students while discussing where and when some dialects seem to be more impactful, comfortable, or appropriate.

Write Less, Say Less

French mathematician and philosopher Blaise Pascal once said in a letter, "I have made this longer than usual because I have not had time to make it shorter" (1657). Taking time to say things more concisely is not only an important skill, but also a helpful practice to hone your understanding of a concept while persevering through a low-stakes challenge. This strategy is deceptively simple. Start with either a shared text or a piece of student writing. Challenge students to cut the length of the text in half, then in half again. Instruct them to rewrite rather than edit, and underscore the goal of preserving any important information. It can be fun to see how low they can go, lengthwise.

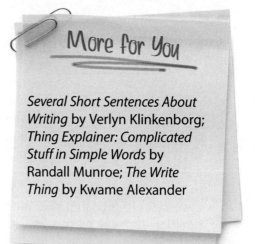

More for You

Several Short Sentences About Writing by Verlyn Klinkenborg; *Thing Explainer: Complicated Stuff in Simple Words* by Randall Munroe; *The Write Thing* by Kwame Alexander

Make It Real

Grades PK–2

- Use this strategy orally with young students. Invite them to practice summarizing stories or information out loud.

- Reverse this strategy by taking the bones of a story and instructing students to fill in details or descriptions using vocabulary words.

Grades 3–5

- Put students in small groups. Invite each group to shorten a different piece of the same nonfiction text, then connect the pieces into a short version of the original. Make sure students take time to review their work and look for key ideas they may have missed.

- Sharing shortened texts as a class, especially if students have worked in groups, can help students discuss the ideas of a text in detail. (Picture Detectives on page 31 may be helpful here, using the questioning/discussion techniques with text instead of a picture.)

Grades 6–12

- This is a helpful strategy for teaching students to write an effective thesis statement, present an argument, or look for a central argument in a text.

- When reading a particularly challenging text, especially a primary source written in an unfamiliar dialect, break the piece into chunks. Have students write a short version of each chunk, then share and discuss.

Keep in Mind

The goal of this strategy is for students to express an idea in their own words, not simply to eliminate words. Providing a "banned word list" of common words from a text may help.

Cardboard Games

Have you ever watched the short documentary "Caine's Arcade" on YouTube? While helping out at his dad's used car parts shop, nine-year-old Caine builds arcade games out of cardboard boxes, packing tape, and whatever else he can find. You can use the same strategy to inspire creativity, reinforce important concepts, and encourage teamwork and celebration. Call around to local shops for discarded cardboard boxes or ask your school custodians to set cardboard aside for you. Students will need some basic guidelines about size and function, but give them as much freedom as possible to imagine and create.

> **More for You**
>
> "Caine's Arcade" documentary by Nirvan Mullick (youtube.com/watch?v=faIFNkdq96U)

Make It Real

Grades PK–2	Grades 3–5	Grades 6–12
• Cardboard games are a fun way to learn about simple machines. Precut or prebuild some pieces, and encourage groups of students to experiment, design, and test games that use a simple machine. • While building, students can also work on geometry concepts. Challenge them to create shapes; for example, use only triangles to make a rectangle or only rectangles to make squares. Or students can learn about concepts such as motion and stability by building something that will make a marble fly into a cup or that will send a marble away and bring it back.	• Upper elementary students can also learn about simple machines using this strategy and can incorporate forces such as gravity, resistance, and momentum into their designs. • Give students a list of pieces or shapes they must use. You can also add measurement limits, such as to perimeter or area, which will compel students to plan and use math.	• Like Escape Room (page 45), this strategy is perfect for homeroom or advisory or any time of day when you need an extra project to bring the group together that can be done a little at a time. • You can use this strategy to work across curriculum, incorporating math and science concepts students are learning as required elements of a game, or creating games themed to history, literature, or language.

Keep in Mind

Depending on the dynamics of your classroom and kids, you may want to allow flexible grouping for this project. For example, you may have a student who has a grand idea they want to do alone or a group of three who will really push each other.

Zines

Zines are just small magazines. They are often handmade and usually focus on a single idea, topic, or point of view. I say "often" and "usually" because there's no right or wrong way to make a zine and no right or wrong zine subject. Zines allow students to share their interests, thoughts, solutions, creations, fandoms, and opinions in a way that is physical and artistic—and doesn't involve counting views or likes.

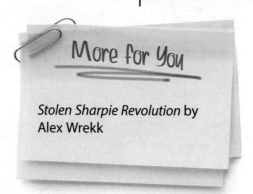

More for You

Stolen Sharpie Revolution by Alex Wrekk

Make It Real

Grades PK–2	Grades 3–5	Grades 6–12
• Give young students plenty of time to plan their zines' topic and appearance before giving them blank, prefolded and prestapled zines to work on. Prepare plenty of extra blanks. Mistakes are an important aspect of making. • A zine is a handy way to collect and send home art, writing, and other work from individual students and the whole class. Many copiers have booklet-making functions to simplify the process.	• When your class is studying a novel, a time period, or famous inventors, scientists, or mathematicians, invite each student to create a zine from the point of view of a specific character, person, or school of thought. • Use zines to capture work done as part of a passion project or as the culmination of a long-term academic goal. Give students space to write and share what they learned, how they learned it, and what growth they achieved over the course of the project or unit.	• Show older students examples of particularly well-done and diverse zines and zine art before they start on their own zines. A brief look at what is possible will help them expand their own goals. • Ask students, "What important thing is never talked about in school?" Each student's zine can be a vehicle for studying, writing about, and sharing their special interests and ideas with classmates in a way that requires planning, clear communication, and an understanding of audience.

Keep in Mind

Zines are fun and engaging in part because they are small and easy to pass around. Zines can also be a pain because they are small and easy to pass around. If your students seem to need it, remind them before and during your zine project not to write or draw anything that could harm their classmates.

Chunky Teaching

Essays are the platform from which I taught many important reading and writing skills. One year, three different students turned in the same fantastic and surprisingly advanced essay about *Romeo and Juliet*. It took me about ten seconds to find that essay online. Those were the days before the rise of AI chatbots and other tools that can write "original," unique—and therefore harder-to-trace—essays. It's a different world now, but the skills my students used to learn while working on long-form essays are still important. You can teach those skills one at a time, presenting smaller chunks of learning in smaller chunks of time so each can be introduced, practiced, and mastered right in class, without AI interference.

More for You

The Perfect Square strategy on page 57 offers another way to chunk learning for students. With each student working on one small square, together they can create a large piece of art.

Make It Real

Grades PK–2	Grades 3–5	Grades 6–12
• When young students seem to be struggling hard on a particular project or lesson, remember the specific learning goal you have and focus on just that goal. For example, if you are doing a project that involves a lot of tracing, cutting, folding, and gluing so students can practice symmetry, you may have students who get so frustrated by the fine-motor tasks that they don't even notice whether both sides of their work look the same. To prevent situations like this, keep your instructions and expectations simple.	• Chunking your teaching is not just a cheating prevention strategy, it's also an effective way for students to tackle complex ideas, difficult texts, and large projects. Lofty goals are wonderful—so long as you help students get there bit by bit. • If you're working on a large research project, tie each piece of it to a specific skill. (For example, tell students that the written summary must show proper use of capital letters and punctuation, the pictures must have sources cited, and so forth.) Focus on these skills one at a time so students don't get overwhelmed.	• Older students must be able to effectively read to learn, write to communicate, critically examine texts, express complex ideas, and complete work that is well organized and presentable. They do not need to do these things all at once all the time. These skills can be broken down, assessed, and mastered individually so you and your students can see where their strengths and challenges are and so you can easily track growth in those areas.

Keep in Mind

Breaking projects into small pieces doesn't mean you're making them easier or slowing them down. In fact, when you isolate skills and lessons, you should have high expectations for student performance.

Idea Books

An idea book is just what it sounds like: a book for ideas, in which a student can write or draw whatever they want. Idea books can be sketchbooks, hardcover journals, or just about any kind of notebook. The most important aspects of this strategy are giving students time and space to use their idea books, providing questions and inspiration they can draw from if they like, and not requiring or assigning anything. (If you must have requirements, you could ask for a certain number of entries over the course of a school term.) Make sure every student understands their idea book is theirs alone—for ideas, sketches, dreams, writing, and decorating.

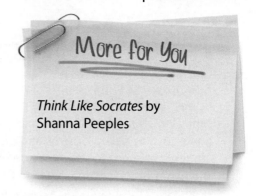

More for You

Think Like Socrates by Shanna Peeples

Make It Real

Grades PK–2	Grades 3–5	Grades 6–12
• Start by having students decorate their idea books with collages of favorite things. Sharing those collages will help students get to know each other and give them a sense of ownership of their idea books. • With young students, you may want to bring out and use the idea books only when the whole class can use them for a similar purpose. Use them as tools specifically for writing or drawing future plans, inventions, story ideas, and so on, rather than as scribble pads for everyday doodling, drawing, and coloring.	• When you present students with their idea books, show them examples from famous thinkers and makers, such as Leonardo da Vinci's notebooks, Octavia Butler's papers, and Jim Henson's sketches. Show students how idea books can look dramatically different. • A wonderful first prompt for an idea book comes from Shanna Peeple's book *Think Like Socrates*. Ask students to list, as many as and fast as they can, the questions that stay with them. (You may need to model a few big philosophical questions first.) Students can refer back to (and change) their lists all year.	• An idea book can help adolescents speak to a world that they may feel isn't listening. Give students prompts asking them to explain or show what they think about different world events, what they would do to fix things if they could, or what they would say if everyone were listening. • When you hand out idea books to students, give them time to plan (in the book) what they want to use it for. Do they have things they would like to do or learn? Something they want to design or plan for? What do they need more space for in their lives?

Keep in Mind

Have a plan for privacy. Let students know that if they leave their idea books lying around, someone may go through them. Encourage students to respect each other's privacy if they do find someone else's idea book.

Prototype Development

A prototype is simply a novel solution to a problem. Give students opportunities to think outside of what is currently possible or typical to strengthen their thinking muscles and help them identify pieces of complex problems and possible solutions. The problems students attempt to solve may be big or small, and you can adapt the parameters for prototypes to fit your class and your lesson goals. Start by showing a few examples of prototypes for common items. Discuss what problems those prototypes tried to solve.

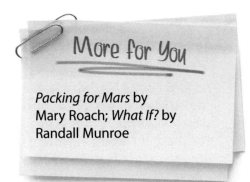

More for You

Packing for Mars by Mary Roach; *What If?* by Randall Munroe

Make It Real

Grades PK–2	Grades 3–5	Grades 6–12
• Before young students start designing, have them think about and discuss what their prototypes will need. For example, if they are designing a ship to go to Mars, what would the ship need to have on it? When the giggling about toilets stops, make sure they have thought through everything humans need to live, then invite them to draw a ship that has all these things. • Get students to talk and think about solutions to problems in their own lives. For example, what could they build to help students clean up after lunch? To make recess equipment use fairer and more fun? To load buses faster at the end of the day?	• See what prototypes students can imagine with limited resources. For example, issue the following challenge: using only simple machines and gravity, design something that could travel underwater or at high speeds, or that could build tall towers. • After sharing a few examples or coming up with a few as a class, have students write their own problems to solve on sheets of paper, then randomly distribute the papers so each student must design a solution for someone else. The problems could be silly (What if squirrels rebelled?) or based on real issues (Shoes should last longer!).	• During a cross-curricular week themed on space travel, my students read a chapter from Mary Roach's book *Packing for Mars* about how hard it is to poop in space, then designed prototypes to address that problem and others that come with trying to do normal things in gravity-free environments. 10/10 would recommend. • What if humans never made a combustion engine or a rubber tire? Let students come up with their own what-ifs or offer options based on what you're studying. They could work on designs for new inventions or show how our world would be different if we had come up with different solutions to common problems.

Keep in Mind

The limits you put on students' prototype designs should depend on what kind of thinking or learning you want them to focus on. Add planning and proposal writing to help them hit your learning goals.

Perfect Square

Kurt Vonnegut wrote that artists are people who understand they can't fix the whole world, but who say, "By golly, I can make this square of canvas, or this eight-and-a-half-by-eleven piece of paper, or this lump of clay, or these twelve bars of music, exactly what they ought to be!" (1998, 162). Use this strategy when a concept, a conversation, or world events are starting to overwhelm all the brains in the room to help reframe feelings, focus on making one small wish, imagine one small fix, or provide a clear example of a complicated topic. Give students squares of blank paper and art supplies, and discuss how small acts can affect big things.

More for You

All You Can Imagine by Bernardo Marçolla

Make It Real

Grades PK–2	Grades 3–5	Grades 6–12
• This strategy complements any lesson on kindness, school citizenship, or public service. Students use their squares to draw their own ideas of what it means to be kind to someone or what they could do to help their community. Squares could be displayed together or wherever they apply. (For example, a square about sharing could be displayed near playground equipment, and a square about cleaning up after yourself could go in the cafeteria.) • As a way to share who they are, each student could decorate a square to show their favorite piece of the world.	• When your students are experiencing a difficult or sad time together, perfect squares can help them deal with big emotions. Use them to send well-wishes, thank-yous, or farewells to a classmate or a staff member in need. To help students make messages that are meaningful and personal, provide prompts (for example, "What is one thing you would like to see if you were sad?" or "What is one nice memory you have with this person?"). • A perfect square can be a window into the future. What does each student see there? How do we get there from here?	• This strategy can be especially helpful after studying or experiencing large and difficult world events. Encourage students to think about small ways in which they can make a positive impact. Provide time to journal or reflect. Examples may be helpful. • If students are struggling to understand a complex system, assign each student (or let each student choose) one piece or example of that system (how laws are passed, or how ecosystems find equilibrium) for their square. Students then assemble their squares on a wall to illustrate the system.

Keep in Mind

Students may or may not feel comfortable sharing what their images represent. If your goals allow, it's okay to let students keep this information private.

Class Congress

Nothing—and I mean nothing—is more interesting to young people than *Robert's Rules of Order*. You have no doubt seen youths in packs wearing T-shirts emblazoned with "I ♥ Parliamentary Procedure" and "I move and ask for unanimous consent." Really, though . . . As I mentioned in You Need a Protocol (page 41), structure is key to having a productive conversation. Help students engage in the complexity of a problem while trying to construct a solution. Have them go through the basic steps of a bill in the US Congress (proposal, committee for study, debate, and vote) with school proposals, current challenges in Congress, or subjects you are studying. A finite budget and multiple bills competing for funding adds an element of mathematics and practicality.

More for You

Teaching Civics Today by John Larmer

Make It Real

Grades PK–2	Grades 3–5	Grades 6–12
• Discuss a recent class issue in a class congress to give students voice and ownership. For example, if the issue is that students are leaving a mess at lunch, groups of students (committees) can propose solutions, which the full congress can then discuss and vote on. • In conjunction with Role-Playing (page 59), students can propose laws for a fictional world or propose rule changes for how the game is played.	• Create a simulation in which the school has a budget for improvements and your students must decide how to use the money. Place students into small-group committees, each with a different focus: food, library, technology, exercise, and so forth. Each committee must present a proposal asking for a certain amount of money. Use a simple version of *Robert's Rules* or another protocol for conducting the debate, and give students time to edit, adjust, and re-propose their ideas.	• The simulation for grades 3–5 can work well for secondary students too. Add the option to form coalitions of committees or to reorganize committees into political parties with specific goals after the funding simulation. • A class congress devoted to the subject you teach can inspire creativity and complex thinking directly related to your learning. For example: Where should scientific funding go? At what age should various rights be granted? Is zero a number? What should we read next?

Keep in Mind

The more work you do establishing and practicing the rules of proposals and debate, the more smoothly and productively the debate will go. It doesn't hurt to add a little theater (see if you can use the school theater or bring in lecterns) to make this activity feel special and different. Your local government representatives may enjoy being invited to speak at, watch, or preside over the session.

Role-Playing

Adventures in Cardboard is a popular Minnesota summer camp. Each week, the campers spend full days immersed in a fantasy role-playing game that spans miles of parkland and includes armor, weapons, magical items, and castles made of cardboard. I've been on nature walks and come across twenty or so small warriors, covered in the dead relatives of the surrounding trees, off to raid another kingdom. It's quite a sight—and a wonderful way to learn. Role-playing games (RPGs) can build skills across subjects, give students engaging and memorable experiences, and create a ton of fun.

More for You

Adventures in Cardboard® (adventuresincardboard.com); Classcraft (classcraft.com); Jonathon Boyle's storytelling games (residentbard.itch.io)

Make It Real

Grades PK–2	Grades 3–5	Grades 6–12
• The heart of role-playing—creating a character, a world, an adventure, and gathering a group to imagine together—is probably already happening on your playground. Add some structure and rules to bring that play into your room and your lessons. • Add number cubes and a storyline to math practice. By using a simplified gaming system (rolls totaling more than six are success, obstacles subtract a certain amount from the total), students can work out math problems (if this door has 3 strength plus 2 protection spell, does your roll break it down?) for hours while searching for treasure or taking cats on an adventure.	• Have you ever seen a role-playing game in process? There is so much math, storytelling, collaboration, and artistry involved. RPGs are not all goblins and violence. Dig a little online or visit your local gaming store to find the right fit for your class. • Have each student draw an avatar and post the avatars on the wall. Avatars could be animals, heroes, or just about anything. Award avatars points for great work or kind actions throughout the day. Points can be spent on outfits, items, or skills to be used during class RPG adventures.	• There are some websites (Classcraft is the one I've seen used most effectively) where students can build and equip avatars, go on adventures, and upgrade abilities. Planning and creativity can bring that kind of experience off screens. Give students character sheets and let your experienced role-playing students lead and do their own maps and scenes. • Some of the most popular online RPGs are simulation games. Players try to become social media stars, farmers, soccer team managers, and even—I kid you not—power-washers. Let students develop their own RPGs based on their special interests or life goals. This can help them develop skills in probability, story building, budgeting, and communication.

Keep in Mind

Awarding experience points (XPs) to avatars is a great way to reward behavior, effort, and action without tying them to a grade.

Gardens

Juliana Urtubey, the 2021 National Teacher of the Year, is on my education Mount Rushmore (along with the two best teachers I've ever known, Ruth and Kristen, and Jim Henson for his work on *Sesame Street*). Juliana taught for many years in Las Vegas, Nevada, and created a community garden with her class. The whole story is incredible, and you should email her and tell her to write a book about it. You should also start thinking about what you would need to start and maintain a garden with your students.

More for You

Jayden's Impossible Garden by Mélina Mangal

Make It Real

Grades PK–2	Grades 3–5	Grades 6–12
• Start your garden indoors, where students can closely watch the plants grow. While tending them, students learn about the stages of seed to full-grown plant and what we give to and get from plant life. Hold a graduation ceremony when the plants are ready to move outside. Ask students, "How does caring for plants change at different stages?" • Give students a snack of fruits and/or vegetables. Afterward, ask what they know about where those foods came from. Show students the seeds that grow into those foods and start a garden where students will, much later, gather and recreate the same snack from seed to table.	• The things that grow around you are part of the history of where you live. Are there foods, flowers, or grasses that used to cover the land you stand on but that your students never or rarely see? Grow these plants with your students while you learn about why they were and are important. • Use your garden to teach the steps of scientific method. For example: What conditions or treatments will grow the largest sunflowers or tastiest tomatoes? How can you design and conduct an experiment to test your hypothesis? What data can you collect, and when and how will you draw your conclusions?	• A garden planned, planted, and tended by your class will strengthen your community, build a sense of inclusion and belonging in the school, and provide a tool to cultivate social and emotional health. • Sections of your garden can serve as time capsules and teaching tools for different times in local history, as well as lessons on what foods are (and were) easily available and affordable in your area.

Keep in Mind

Every garden involves failure. Plants may grow poorly or not at all, squirrels will be squirrels, watering may be forgotten on the day before a long break. These are great opportunities to talk with students about failure as an important part of learning. Finding examples of garden fails to share with them may be fun and helpful as well.

Plan a Day, Plan the Future

The goal of this strategy is to help students conceptualize time in a more physical way, reflect on how they spend their time, and plan how they could use their time differently in the future. The idea behind this strategy comes from Tim Urban, writer of the website Wait But Why. His "100 Blocks a Day" post is a fascinating way to understand how you spend time, plan for ideal days, or look at how you can change your routines to match your future goals. It's a quick read, and I recommend it, but the central point is that people tend to have about one thousand minutes a day (or one hundred ten-minute chunks) that they spend awake. You start your day with these hundred blocks and spend them as you go through the day in a variety of ways.

More for You

Wait But Why (waitbutwhy. com); *Creative Hustle* by Olatunde Sobomehin and sam seidel

Make It Real

Grades PK–2	Grades 3–5	Grades 6–12
• One hundred blocks and a full day is probably too much for young children to start with. Give students enough blank spaces or manipulatives to reflect their whole day at school to color-code or physically lay out their schedule to get them thinking about time as a unit of measurement.	• Using a large grid of one hundred squares (or any manipulative that works for you), have students try to map out how they spend a typical day versus how they would spend a "perfect" day.	• With practices, clubs, activities, social and family time, and full school days to manage, adolescents may feel like they have far too many things to do and not nearly enough time to do them. Use this strategy to help students see if they are spending their according to their priorities.
• Give students access to different-colored blocks that represent different subjects or activities: math, reading, exercise, sports, screen time, and so on. Ask students, "How would you like to spend your day? Show it with the blocks."	• When students are comfortable in the practice of using a grid (or blocks, or however you want them to represent the chunks of their day), have them use this strategy to plan what they will do during work time on a project or how they will get a big task done. (For example, say, "This project will take about ten blocks to finish. When will you spend them?")	• As students start to plan for their futures, this strategy can get them to imagine an "ideal" day (not a dream day full of lottery winning and celebrity dates, but a realistic day in their hoped-for future life) and understand how their current actions support that plan (or don't).

Keep in Mind

One of the hardest things for students to estimate effectively is screen time. Have students track or look up their screen time before introducing this activity.

Self-Portrait

There are many ways to create self-portraits and many reasons to create them. They can help your students explore and share where your they come from and where they are going. Depending on your goals, think about how a self-portrait can show two or more sides, how it can show external and internal characteristics, and how it needn't be a picture of a student's appearance.

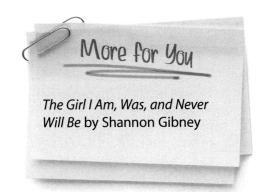

More for You

The Girl I Am, Was, and Never Will Be by Shannon Gibney

Make It Real

Grades PK–2	Grades 3–5	Grades 6–12
• Student self-portraits of future selves (in one year or ten), in a favorite place, or doing something they'd like to learn one day are a great way to get students talking about their interests and aspirations. • A self-portrait can take a variety of forms. Give each student an outline of a child's body. Inside that outline, students can add images of their favorite foods, who they live with, and other key aspects of who they are.	• Give each student (or have them create) an outline of a person. Outside the outline, they can draw, write, or collage images of the world outside themselves. On the inside, they can use images and words to represent who they are. • Invite students to design a logo or crest that represents who they are. Provide a list of common symbols and their meanings. Final versions can be made into buttons or iron-on patches or displayed in the room.	• Have students create split portraits to explore individual and cultural identities. Students create self-portraits with one half representing their family or culture and one half representing their individual characteristics and passions. Split portraits are a helpful way to get to know one another at the start of the year. • Using layers of paper, students create multiple portraits showing what others see about them and what others don't or can't see.

Keep in Mind

Talking about personal identity can bring up all sorts of feelings for students, depending on their experiences, life and family situations, and self-image. Model this strategy, showing some vulnerability, before inviting students to try it.

Identity Bubble Map

Bubble maps can help students draw connections within complex ideas. Students can map relationships among real and fictional people or places and among ideas in the communities they are part of. Bubble maps are especially helpful for mapping the internal world of who students are, how they learn, what they have experienced, where they are from, and why all those elements affect the way students see the world.

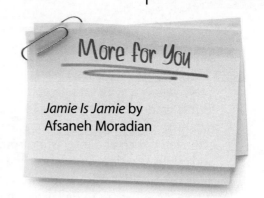

More for You

Jamie Is Jamie by Afsaneh Moradian

Make It Real

Grades PK–2	Grades 3–5	Grades 6–12
• Give each student a page of empty bubbles to fill in with words, images, or some combination. Then have students share with each other as a way to learn about their classmates. • Create a classwide identity map together. You can give each student a piece of the classroom they can decorate to represent themself. Or you can create large bubbles that show a variety of likes, dislikes, talents, and hobbies, and invite students to add their names to the ones they share.	• Have each student create a two-sided identity map of their internal and external self, then share their map with other students to get to know each other, talk about their interests and experiences, and make connections. • When students have the concept down, identity maps can also be used for people or characters you are studying. What do students know about the people or characters? What can they guess?	• Identity maps are useful preparation tools before starting a lesson that includes concepts such as bias, perspective, or conflict. When students make and share maps of how their own perceptions have been shaped, they can better understand how others' perceptions may be different. • Multiple maps or split maps give students a concrete way to examine different aspects of their identities depending on where they are, who they are with, or who they plan to be. Ask students to make three different maps of their choosing (all related to themselves in some way).

Keep in Mind

Let students take the lead on the content of their identity maps. There may be things they don't want to share with everyone, or there may be things that others see in them that they don't find to be important.

Interviews

Every year, a teacher at one of my old schools would have her fourth graders ask ten people in their lives, "What is the very first historic event you remember happening?" This assignment often led to rich and interesting conversations between students and adults throughout the building and within students' families and communities. People around the world are more connected than ever, yet seem to be talking to each other less. Conducting interviews is a fun way to build communication skills and think critically about how memory, perspective, context, and experience can affect what people say and hear in conversation.

More for You

Humans of New York by Brandon Stanton (humansofnewyork.com)

Make It Real

Grades PK–2	Grades 3–5	Grades 6–12
• Use interviews to introduce your students to the other adults at school, all of whom are there to help students. Invite your school's nurse, librarian, paras, front office staff, food service staff, and others to visit your classroom. Have students interview staff about who they are, what they do, and what they like. • Have students interview adults who are important parts of their lives at home or in their community and then share those interviews with the class.	• Take your students out into the community around the school. Contact an elder-care facility or put out a call for local volunteers to visit your class and talk about their careers or cultures to help your students build a more complex understanding of their world. (See also Map Your World on page 30.) • Pair interviews (original or researched) with nonfiction texts on the same topic to provide rich material for analyzing what is missing or different between written perspectives on the same event.	• As students discover their passions and career plans, they can reach out to adults who are already doing that work. It's a good idea for you, as the teacher, to supervise the communication, but talking with someone successful in a particular field can be a life-changing experience for students. • Teach students etiquette around asking for and conducting interviews, being mindful of others' time, and recognizing how many such requests they may get.

Keep in Mind

When assigning interviews, be aware that not all your students may have access to family members, technology, or community events. Give students multiple options and ways to complete the work. Offer some in-school options, such as video calling with members of your own network.

Write a Picture Book

If you, like me, ever thought that children's books must be easy to write, I implore you to try writing one. I will not share the disastrous results of my attempts, but they taught me that writing a great picture book is challenging. It requires economy of words, vibrancy of images, and clarity of ideas—and that's why writing a picture book is an excellent learning project across many subjects. To write a picture book on a topic, students must stop and think about what is essential to learn about that topic and how they can convey that information simply. Offer plenty of examples and templates to get students started.

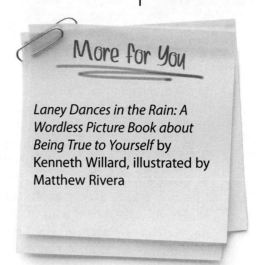

More for You

Laney Dances in the Rain: A Wordless Picture Book about Being True to Yourself by Kenneth Willard, illustrated by Matthew Rivera

Make It Real

Grades PK–2	Grades 3–5	Grades 6–12
• Show young students a few examples of wordless picture books that tell a story. Give each student a planning sheet to sketch out their own wordless story before working on a final draft. Adults or older student helpers can write words for the students if needed. • Giving students only words or only pictures from a story can help them creatively storytell or work on observation, inference, and other skills.	• Not every student picture book needs to be a polished, finished draft—especially if the thinking involved in creating the book is the most important goal. Have each student create a rough version of a picture book that will explain a topic to another student. Then have them review their work to see where they may need to gather more information or where they were unsure of what to say.	• Many excellent picture books are intended for older audiences, playing on the genre in way that secondary students will have fun emulating. Invite students to assess and share their learning through writing picture books. This effort will help students identify what they've learned well enough to express in new ways.

Keep in Mind

It's wonderful to have beautiful, polished final picture books. However, if the goal is the thinking and planning involved, it's just fine if they don't turn out perfectly.

Topical Storm

In need of a community-building, warm-up, or homeroom activity? This is one of my favorites because it works when it's highly structured and directed *and* when it devolves into chaos. Have students sit with stacks of small sheets of paper, on which they write topics for discussion, interesting questions, ridiculous statistics, random objects, or whatever focus you choose. Then they crumple up all their papers into balls and, at the designated moment, create a storm of topics. Where you take it next is up to you. Concentric circles of one-on-one conversations? Fishbowl? Small groups? Your room is ready for lots of simultaneous discussions among students whose brains are already activated and who have a wealth of surprise topics literally at their feet.

More for You

How (and Why) to Get Students Talking by Jean Sunde Peterson

Make It Real

Grades PK–2	Grades 3–5	Grades 6–12
• You can make this strategy a lot less dependent on each student's ability to write and read by supplying sheets with a variety of images related to the discussion you'd like to have (favorites, thinking about the future, or reviewing letters, sounds, math problems, and so forth). Students can still create a "storm," walk around the room finding new partners, and pick up topics from the floor.	• You may want to lay down some ground rules about topics, as only so many conversations can be had about the word *poop*. • This strategy works well for reviewing material learned in class. The questions are anonymous, so students can ask questions about what they are struggling with. Have students stand in a circle and, if they know the answer, jump in the middle to explain.	• Students carry all sorts of protective shells with them through their day. Sometimes, those shells can prevent them from talking to people outside their friend circle, or can lead them to assume too much about each other. Strategies like this, which help students start conversations and look for connections afterward, build a stronger community. As trust grows, you can focus topics on more personal questions.

Keep in Mind

Random and surprise topics can be fun, but you also want to make sure students can opt out of a topic they don't want to talk about. One advantage of there being so many on the floor is that students can easily drop (into the trash if necessary) any topic that would be uncomfortable. A short conversation beforehand about thinking about classmates before writing down anything intentionally edgy or offensive goes a long way.

Read a Book Out Loud

Sharing a text gives your class an artifact to focus on for discussion. Students of any age can illustrate or investigate ideas in all the picture books recommended in the preceding strategies. Choose a high-interest book to read aloud every day or every few days, one chunk at a time, to expose students to great literature and to novels they may struggle to read alone. There's also this: literature is the most common form of art students encounter at school, and nothing brings out the power and purpose of art like sharing it with others. So, take a book—pretty much any book—and read it out loud.

More for You

When you finish one book, you can read a different book, also out loud.

Make It Real

Grades PK–2	Grades 3–5	Grades 6–8
• Read a book out loud.	• Choose a book and read it out loud.	• Read a book out loud.

Keep in Mind

When reading the book, do it out loud.

References

Appleby, Drew C. 2017. "The Soft Skills College Students Need to Succeed Now and in the Future." American Psychological Association. September 2017. apa.org/ed/precollege/psn/2017/09/soft-skills.

Ben-Yehudah, Gal, and Adi Brann. 2019. "Pay Attention to Digital Text: The Impact of the Media on Text Comprehension and Self-Monitoring in Higher-Education Students with ADHD." *Research in Developmental Disabilities* 89: 120–129. doi.org/10.1016/j.ridd.2019.04.001.

Cipriano, Christina, Michael J. Strambler, Lauren H. Naples, Cheyeon Ha, Megan Kirk, Miranda Wood, Kaveri Sehgal, et al. 2023. "Stage 2 Report: The State of the Evidence for Social and Emotional Learning: A Contemporary Meta-Analysis of Universal School–Based SEL Interventions." OSF Preprints. February 2, 2023. doi.org/10.31219/osf.io/mk35u.

Davidesco, Ido, Emma Laurent, Henry Valk, Tessa West, Catherine Milne, David Poeppel, and Suzanne Dikker. 2023. "The Temporal Dynamics of Brain-to-Brain Synchrony Between Students and Teachers Predict Learning Outcomes." *Psychological Science* 34 (5): 633–643. doi.org/10.1177/09567976231163872.

Denworth, Lydia. 2023. "Brain Waves Synchronize When People Interact." *Scientific American* 329 (1): 50. scientificamerican.com/article/brain-waves-synchronize-when-people-interact.

Ding, Keya, and Hui Li. 2023. "Digital Addiction Intervention for Children and Adolescents: A Scoping Review." *International Journal of Environmental Research and Public Health* 20 (6): 4777. doi.org/10.3390/ijerph20064777.

Dwyer, Christopher P. 2023. "An Evaluative Review of Barriers to Critical Thinking in Educational and Real-World Settings." *Journal of Intelligence* 11 (6): 105. doi.org/10.3390/jintelligence11060105.

Furenes, Mary Irene, Natalia Kucirkova, and Adriana G. Bus. 2021. "A Comparison of Children's Reading on Paper Versus Screen: A Meta-Analysis." *Review of Educational Research* 91 (4): 483–517. doi.org/10.3102/0034654321998074.

Gray, Peter, David F. Lancy, and David F. Bjorklund. 2023. "Decline in Independent Activity as a Cause of Decline in Children's Mental Well-being: Summary of the Evidence." *Journal of Pediatrics* 260. doi.org/10.1016/j.jpeds.2023.02.004.

Gruber, Matthias J., Ashvanti Valji, and Charan Ranganath. 2017. "Curiosity and Learning: A Neuroscientific Perspective." In *The Cambridge Handbook of Motivation and Learning*, edited by K. Ann Redinger and Suzanne E. Hidi, 397–417. Cambridge, UK: Cambridge University Press.

Horowitz-Kraus, Tzipi, and John S. Hutton. 2018. "Brain Connectivity in Children Is Increased by the Time They Spend Reading Books and Decreased by the Length of Exposure to Screen-Based Media." *Acta Paediatrica* 107 (4): 685–693. doi.org/10.1111/apa.14176.

Jenkins, Henry. 2009. *Confronting the Challenges of Participatory Culture: Media Education for the 21st Century.* Cambridge, MA: MIT Press.

Kanov, Jason M., Sally Maitlis, Monica C. Worline, Jane E. Dutton, Peter J. Frost, and Jacoba M. Lilius. 2004. "Compassion in Organizational Life." *American Behavioral Scientist* 47 (6): 808–827. doi.org/10.1177/0002764203260.

Klein, Alyson. 2021. "During COVID-19, Schools Have Made a Mad Dash to 1-to-1 Computing. What Happens Next?" *Education Week*, April 20, 2021. edweek.org/technology/during-covid-19-schools-have-made-a-mad-dash-to-1-to-1-computing-what-happens-next/2021/04.

Koedinger, Kenneth R., Julie L. Booth, and David Klahr. 2013. "Instructional Complexity and the Science to Constrain It." *Science* 342: 935–937. doi.org/10.1126/science.1238056.

Loewenstein, George. 1994. "The Psychology of Curiosity: A Review and Reinterpretation." *Psychological Bulletin* 116 (1): 75–98. doi.org/10.1037/0033-2909.116.1.75.

Mascaro, Jennifer S., Marianne P. Florian, Marcia J. Ash, Patricia K. Palmer, Tyralynn Frazier, Paul Condon, and Charles Raison. 2020. "Ways of Knowing Compassion: How Do We Come to Know, Understand, and Measure Compassion When We See It?" *Frontiers in Psychology* 2020 Oct. 2 (11): 547241. doi.org/10.3389/fpsyg.2020.547241.

OECD. 2019. "OECD Future of Education and Skills 2030: Conceptual Learning Framework—Skills for 2030." oecd.org/education/2030-project/teaching-and-learning/learning/skills/Skills_for_2030_concept_note.pdf.

Partnership for 21st Century Learning. 2015. "P21 Framework Definitions." May 2015. static.battelleforkids.org/documents/p21/P21_Framework_Definitions_New_Logo_2015_9pgs.pdf.

Pascal, Blaise. 1657. *Lettres Provinciales No. 16.* In *Oxford Essential Quotations*, edited by Susan Ratcliffe, 2017. Oxford, UK: Oxford University Press.

Rau, Martina A. 2017. "How do Students Learn to See Concepts in Visualizations? Social Learning Mechanisms with Physical and Virtual Representations." *Journal of Learning Analytics* 4 (2): 240–263. doi.org/10.18608/jla.2017.42.16.

Southworth, James. 2022. "Bridging Critical Thinking and Transformative Learning: The Role of Perspective-Taking." *Theory and Research in Education* 20 (1): 44–63. doi.org/10.1177/14778785221090853.

Styers, Mary. 2022. "EdTech Top 40 Report Shares the Latest on the Usage of Digital Tools during the 2021–22 School Year." *Instructure*, August 24, 2022. instructure.com/resources/blog/edtech-top-40-report-shares-latest-usage-digital-tools-during-2021-22-school-year.

Thakral, Preston P., Amanda C. Yang, Donna Rose Addis, and Daniel L. Schacter. 2021. "Divergent Thinking and Constructing Future Events: Dissociating Old from New Ideas." *Memory* 29 (6): 729–743. doi.org/10.1080/09658211.2021.1940205.

Vonnegut, Kurt. 1998. *Timequake.* London: Vintage.

William and Flora Hewlett Foundation. 2013. "Deeper Learning Competencies." April 2013. hewlett.org/wp-content/uploads/2016/08/Deeper_Learning_Defined__April_2013.pdf.

World Economic Forum. 2023. "Future of Jobs Report 2023." April 30, 2023. weforum.org/reports/the-future-of-jobs-report-2023.

Zivan, Michal, Sasson Vaknin, Nimrod Peleg, Rakefet Ackerman, and Tzipi Horowitz-Kraus. 2023. "Higher Theta-Beta Ratio during Screen-Based vs. Printed Paper Is Related to Lower Attention in Children: An EEG Study." *PLOS ONE* 18 (5): e0283863. doi.org/10.1371/journal.pone.0283863.

Sample Lessons

Lesson: "Letter from Birmingham Jail"

This lesson is best suited to secondary students but is adaptable to lower grades.

Part 1: Activating Background Knowledge
Strategy: Picture Detectives (page 31)

1. Show students the following image (a partial photo showing just the firefighters). Using the Picture Detectives strategy, ask students what's happening in the picture, what makes them think that, and what more they can find. This isn't about guessing correctly or incorrectly about the picture's subject; rather, it's about looking for details and clues to get students thinking and talking.

2. After a few minutes of discussion, reveal the following complete photo, showing protesters being attacked by the firehose. Tell the class it's okay to see the same details differently now, with new information, and restart the discussion.

3. Finish this activity by asking students what they know, what they think they know, and what they have questions about regarding the US civil rights movement.

Part 2: Context

Strategies: Zines (page 53), Chunky Teaching (page 54), One-Pagers (page 19), Museum of Ideas (page 24)

1. The amount of context you want to share before you start reading Dr. Martin Luther King Jr.'s "Letter from Birmingham Jail" is up to you. In my last school, students had read *The Watsons Go to Birmingham—1963* two years earlier, so they were able to make many connections once they had a chance to recall it and activate their background knowledge.

2. If your class needs more context about the civil rights movement—especially if they have only heard of King and Rosa Parks—any of the strategies mentioned above can help students spend an hour, a day, or a week seeking out untold stories, new perspectives, and other important context. You could also use Part 5 of this lesson here and focus on the civil rights movement period.

Part 3: Letter Excerpt

Strategies: Collaborative Reading (page 40), Historical Primary Sources (page 21)

1. Before handing out excerpts of King's "Letter from Birmingham Jail" (see activity sheet on pages 72–73), let students know that they will be reading something important—an actual piece of history—and they will be reading it multiple times. Students may find it interesting or engaging to know that instead of reading *about* King, they will be reading his actual words—some of which may be surprising.

2. When I taught this lesson, I added the Collaborative Reading directions and some brief historical context to an excerpt of King's letter, but you may prefer to simply give students the text and facilitate the reading in your own way. The key is to give students time to read the document closely, to read it multiple times, and to share what they are thinking, questioning, and learning as they read.

Part 4: Application

Strategy: Perfect Square (page 57)

1. The Perfect Square strategy asks students to imagine one part of the world exactly as it should be. This strategy works well as students are tackling King's ideas about being "creative extremists" for "love, truth, and justice."

2. Have students use that strategy and focus it specifically on the kind of work they want to do in the world to make it better. It doesn't need to be political work in nature. This helps students think about themselves as active participants in the world in big and small ways.

3. Make sure to give students time to brainstorm and sketch before giving them squares of paper and materials. There's also a line in the "Letter from Birmingham Jail," "Let him march . . . and try to understand why he must do so," that is worth discussing first to show students they don't need to agree with each other in order to understand why issues may be important to students they share the class with.

Part 5: Extension

Strategy: Museum of Ideas (page 24)

1. Of course, "Letter from Birmingham Jail" can be read at any point of the year, but you may find that your students are ready for this work and conversation around February, during Black History Month. Consider timing this lesson so the walking museum (see student activity sheet on page 75) occurs in February.

2. Get creative with the location for your walking museum. For example, during the first year back in person after COVID lockdowns, students in my district were in the buildings but not using their lockers—so we used those empty lockers to create museum exhibits.

"Letter from Birmingham Jail"

Guess What?

We're going to read something that is super important, so we're going to read it closely. It's the sort of thing you need to read a few times and really dig into. It's worth it, because it's beautiful and important, and because most people never spend the time to really read important work by people they admire.

1. Read Dr. Martin Luther King Jr.'s "Letter from Birmingham Jail" once. Note any words you are unsure about by adding a question mark after the word.

2. As a group, go through the questioned words one by one. See if you can figure out the definitions by looking at the nearby words and with what you already know. Look up the words if needed, but write the definitions in the margins in your own words.

3. Read the passage again, this time looking for words and phrases that tell you what King's main idea is. What is he saying? How do you know? Highlight these words or circle them.

Background

The Birmingham campaign began on April 3, 1963, with coordinated marches and sit-ins against racism and racial segregation in Birmingham, Alabama. On April 12, law enforcement officers arrested King roughly, along with other marchers, while thousands looked on. King was given unusually harsh conditions in Birmingham Jail. An ally smuggled in an April 12 newspaper, which contained "A Call for Unity"—a joint statement by eight white Alabama clergymen against King and his methods. The letter provoked King, and he began to write a response on the newspaper itself.

Excerpts from "Letter from Birmingham Jail" by Dr. Martin Luther King Jr.

Source: King, Martin Luther Jr. 1963. "Letter from a Birmingham Jail." African Studies Center—University of Pennsylvania. africa.upenn.edu/Articles_Gen/Letter_Birmingham.html.

"I cannot sit idly by in Atlanta and not be concerned about what happens in Birmingham. Injustice anywhere is a threat to justice everywhere. . . . Anyone who lives inside the United States can never be considered an outsider anywhere within its bounds."

"We should never forget that everything Adolf Hitler did in Germany was 'legal.' . . . It was 'illegal' to aid and comfort a Jew in Hitler's Germany. Even so, I am sure that, had I lived in Germany at the time, I would have aided and comforted my Jewish brothers. If today I lived in a Communist country where certain principles dear to the Christian faith are suppressed, I would openly advocate disobeying that country's anti-religious laws."

"I must confess that over the past few years I have been gravely disappointed with the white moderate. I have almost reached the regrettable conclusion that the Negro's great stumbling block in his stride toward freedom is not the White Citizen's Counciler or the Ku Klux Klanner, but the white moderate, who is more devoted to 'order' than to justice; who prefers a negative peace which is the absence of tension to a positive peace which is the presence of justice; who constantly says: 'I agree with you in the goal you seek, but I cannot agree with your methods of direct action'; who paternalistically believes he can set the timetable for another man's freedom; who lives by a mythical concept of time and who constantly advises the Negro to wait for a 'more convenient season.'"

Name: _____ Date: _____

"Shallow understanding from people of good will is more frustrating than absolute misunderstanding from people of ill will. Lukewarm acceptance is much more bewildering than outright rejection."

"Oppressed people cannot remain oppressed forever. . . . If one recognizes this vital urge that has engulfed the Negro community, one should readily understand why public demonstrations are taking place. The Negro has many pent up resentments and latent frustrations, and he must release them. So let him march; let him make prayer pilgrimages to the city hall; let him go on freedom rides—and try to understand why he must do so."

"And now this approach is being termed extremist. But though I was initially disappointed at being categorized as an extremist, as I continued to think about the matter I gradually gained a measure of satisfaction from the label. Was not Jesus an extremist for love: 'Love your enemies, bless them that curse you, do good to them that hate you, and pray for them which despitefully use you, and persecute you.' . . . And Abraham Lincoln: 'This nation cannot survive half slave and half free.' And Thomas Jefferson: 'We hold these truths to be self evident, that all men are created equal. . . .'"

"So the question is not whether we will be extremists, but what kind of extremists we will be. Will we be extremists for hate or for love? Will we be extremists for the preservation of injustice or for the extension of justice? In that dramatic scene on Calvary's hill three men were crucified."

"We must never forget that all three were crucified for the same crime—the crime of extremism. Two were extremists for immorality, and thus fell below their environment. The other, Jesus Christ, was an extremist for love, truth and goodness, and thereby rose above his environment. Perhaps the South, the nation and the world are in dire need of creative extremists."

4. Look for lines of this letter that feel important, meaningful, or beautiful to you. Circle or highlight these lines in ways that are impossible to miss.

5. Look for connections between King's letter and your life, find articles from today that match King's letter in some way, or say what some lines make you think. This is your document. Write all over it.

Perfect Square

"So the question is not whether we will be extremists, but what kind of extremists we will be. Will we be extremists for hate or for love? Will we be extremists for the preservation of injustice or for the extension of justice? . . . Perhaps . . . the nation and the world are in dire need of extremists."

Source: King, Martin Luther Jr. 1963. "Letter from a Birmingham Jail." African Studies Center—University of Pennsylvania. africa.upenn.edu/Articles_Gen/Letter_Birmingham.html.

In his "Letter from Birmingham Jail," King talks about the need for people to be "extremists." That may sound like a scary idea, but it's important to understand what King means by the word. To him, an extremist is someone who's moved to action, who believes they must change the world. He also talks about what it means to be a "moderate" in a time of injustice or suffering: it means believing injustice or suffering is bad but not wanting to do anything to fix it.

In front of you is a square of paper. Before you write or draw on it, think about the questions King asks in his letter. What kind of extremist will you be? In other words, what do you want to do to change the world?

You can choose what you put in the square in front of you. Think of it as your piece of the world. How do you want to change it? What do you think people should do, know, or experience? You may want to draw a picture or write a poem or story or speech. Or maybe you think the world needs more beauty, more laughter, more compassion. What can you draw or write that inspires that emotion or expresses that want?

Sketch Your Ideas

When you are done, you will have a chance to share with the class as much as you'd like to about your square, and then we will display the squares for everyone to see and think about.

Name: _____ Date: _____

Black History Month Walking Museum

Goal: Each student will create a display that celebrates a person, event, movement, or moment in Black History.

Your display *must* include:

- at least one primary source document related to your topic
- an analysis of that primary source that explains its context or importance or points out interesting parts
- three visuals
- a list of resources where you found your information

Your display *can* include:

- QR codes to more information, videos, music, and so on
- timelines
- graphs, charts, or infographics
- writing
- any creative display options you can think of

Step 1: Identify a Topic

- Try not to choose something you've heard about or done before. There are millions of possible topics that you could explore for this project.
- Think about important people, places, art, music, politics, science, fashion, or any other part of society. Maybe start with something you are interested in.

Step 2: Research

- Read, watch documentaries, listen to podcasts, interview people—and search deeper than just your topic name. What else was happening during that time? Who were the people around? What impact can we see today? What led to this? As you notice terms or people that keep popping up in your research, or ideas, places, or people you are unfamiliar with, look those up too.
- Keep track of your information and where you found it. When you find something interesting, write it down.
- Find a primary source document (something written at the time by people who were there, such as a speech, law, letter, or journal) related to the topic.

Step 3: Create

- Think about what would make people want to view and read your display.
- Make sure you are spelling words correctly in your display.
- Find or make compelling images.
- Don't just copy a bunch of text. Most of your display should be in your own words. Remember that most museums use display writing that is short, interesting, and informative.

Lesson: Drawing and Connecting

This lesson is best suited to PK–5 but is adaptable to secondary grades. It was created by Jonathan Juravich, 2018 Ohio Teacher of the Year, 2023 National Elementary Art Teacher of the Year, and host of the Emmy-winning digital series *Drawing with Mr. J.* (Reprinted with permission.)

Part 1: The Lesson

Blind Contour Drawing

1. Introduce blind contour drawing to the class: "The name of this drawing practice describes the process: *blind*, meaning 'can't see,' and *contour*, which comes from French, and means 'outline.' So, a blind contour drawing is a 'can't-see line drawing.' The goal of this type of drawing is to focus on your observation skills. Instead of making assumptions, you must stop, look, and notice." A few key points:

   - This experience does not require a blindfold or keeping one's eyes closed while drawing. It simply means not looking at the paper while drawing.

   - The artist looks at their subject with all their attention to learn more about what is in front of them.

   - The result is less important than what the artist learns through the practice of truly observing the subject.

2. Model the process: Demonstrate to students the creation of your own blind contour drawing, talking through your actions as the students watch you create a portrait of a student or another adult in the room. Model vulnerability: because you're not looking at the paper, the students will see the results of your efforts before you do, and there will be lots of giggles—tell students you're okay with that. Talk through what it feels like to study someone else thoroughly, fight the urge to look at the paper, and not worry about the final result.

3. Invite students to try, starting with portraits: Distribute drawing materials (markers are best at first) and paper. Pair students up and have them take turns drawing one another. Ask them to imagine that their eyes and their markers are connected. As their eyes look at their subjects they move the marker slowly across the paper. The key is *slowly*. This process is not a race, and the more time and detail included in the drawing, the more exciting the results will be.

4. Remind students to look at their partners and not at their papers when they're drawing. The subjects can monitor the artists as they watch the drawings unfold. Each artist should draw only what they see, using a single continuous line. That is: once they start drawing, the artist shouldn't pick up their marker until they have reached the end of their drawing. The students should not focus on where they are placing an eyeball or a mouth but instead on capturing the essence of the person they are drawing. Ultimately, the drawing might look like a bunch of spaghetti noodles, and that is okay. There is beauty in those lines, but sometimes students need to hear from their teacher how interesting and exciting their work really is. Walk around the room and celebrate what you see and the bravery it takes to engage with this process while challenging your students to look closer and add more details.

5. When the drawing is complete, both the artist and their subject can laugh about the drawing, celebrate the linework, and discuss how challenging the process may have seemed. Then it is time for the students to switch roles. This switching can continue multiple times throughout the course of the class, or you may want to include some of the following challenges or modifications:

   - Set a timer. The artist must keep drawing and including more and more detail until the timer stops. They are not allowed to finish early.

- Challenge students to draw themselves. Give each student a stand-up mirror to place in front of their paper while drawing. This allows students to look at themselves without seeing their drawing until they are finished.

- Draw objects instead of people—such as potted plants, bouquets of flowers, or other interesting items.

- Invite students to color their drawings to transform the jumbles of lines into accurate representations of their subjects. Or students can use arbitrary colors to fill in the spaces created by the crossing lines, turning their drawings into abstract representations of their subjects.

When the drawings are done, students can keep and cherish or recycle them. Remind students that this lesson is about the process, not the product. Not all the drawings will spark pride or will be desirable to keep, and that is a critical part of the activity. This does not mean students should dismiss their efforts or learning. The goals of the lesson are to slow down, to observe, and to be open to possibilities.

Part 2: The Remixes

Now that students have practice doing blind contour drawings, they can mix this approach with various strategies from this book to connect with each other while deepening their learning or as part of a larger unit on identity, engineering, or social studies. In the following remixes, instead of students simply looking at their subjects, they will talk through topics while they draw, looking only at the people with whom they are conversing (and not at their papers).

Strategy: Self-Portrait (page 62)

Pair up students and have them take turns in the artist and subject roles. While the subject tells the artist about themselves, focusing on things like interests, places they've been, or their family, the artist tries to draw as many of the things described without drawing the subject's face. Afterward, the artist can share their drawing with the subject, explaining the things they chose to draw. After both partners have had a turn in both roles, each can take the other's drawing and use pieces of it to create a self-portrait.

Strategy: Prototype Development (page 56)

Present the class with an image representing a problem they need to "fix" with a prototype drawing of a solution. The representation could be a photo of a river that floods, a machine missing key pieces, a stadium full of people who all want to get home at once, or any image that connects to a topic you are already studying. While looking only at the problem image, students draw a representation of an engineering solution. When they are done drawing, students pass their art around the room and look for ideas and inspiration from each other.

Strategy: Map Your World (page 30)

Pair up students and have them take turns in the speaker and listener roles. To practice using maps and giving directions, have the speaker give directions from one place to another (in the school, neighborhood, or other familiar place) to the listener. The listener tries to draw a map (without looking at the paper) that reflects what they are hearing. After both partners have had a turn in both roles, students can share and explain their maps, then create their own maps of the area they described using their partners' contour drawings as models or guides to inform clarifications.

Digital Resources

The sample lessons and a fillable PDF of each form are available on TCM Content Cloud.

Accessing the Digital Resources

The digital resources can be downloaded by following these steps:

1. Go to www.tcmpub.com/digital

2. Use the 13-digit ISBN number to redeem the digital resources.

3. Respond to the question using the book.

4. Follow the prompts on the Content Cloud website to sign in or create a new account.

5. The content redeemed will appear on your My Content screen. Click on the product to look through the digital resources. All file resources are available for download. Select files can be previewed, opened, and shared. Any web-based content, such as videos, links, or interactive text, can be viewed and used in the browser but is not available for download.

For questions and assistance with your ISBN redemption, please contact Teacher Created Materials..

email: customerservice@tcmpub.com

phone: 800-858-7339